CASE STUDIES ON EDUCATIONAL ADMINISTRATION

CASE STUDIES ON EDUCATIONAL ADMINISTRATION

Theodore J. Kowalski

Teachers College
Ball State University

Longman
New York & London

Case Studies on Educational Administration

Longman, 95 Church Street, White Plains, N.Y. 10601

Associated companies:
Longman Group Ltd., London
Longman Cheshire Pty., Melbourne
Longman Paul Pty., Auckland
Copp Clark Pitman, Toronto

Senior editor: Naomi Silverman
Development editor: Virginia L. Blanford
Production editor: Ann P. Kearns
Cover design: Anne M. Pompeo

Library of Congress Cataloging-in-Publication Data

Kowalski, Theodore J.
    Case studies on educational administration / Theodore J. Kowalski,

       p.   cm.
    Includes bibliographical references and index.
ISBN 0-8013-0387-7
      1. School management and organization—United States—Case
studies. I. Title.
LB2805.K63 1991   90-41080
371.2'00973—dc20   CIP

ABCDEFGHIJ-DO-99 98 97 96 95 94 93 92 91 90

Contents

Preface

During the 1980s, public education was subjected to extreme political scrutiny. Dozens of reform reports criticized the failures of teachers, administrators, and schools. Legislatures were moved to enact intensification mandates and teacher educators scrambled to improve curricula and practices in colleges of education. Amidst this meliorism, there emerged cogent questions relative to the role of school administrators and the professional education of individuals who will occupy these positions.

For decades, graduate study in educational administration appeared to be mired in a debate over the values of theory and practical knowledge. One side argued that the purpose of graduate study is the acquisition of theoretical knowledge while the other proposed that it was the transmission of practical knowledge. During the past decade, there has been a growing recognition that both sides are correct—and that both sides are wrong. The practice of school administration is both a science and an art. It involves theoretical knowledge as well as craft knowledge. It requires technical skills as well as reflective thinking and problem-solving skills. Thus, contemporary reform efforts no longer seek to choose between theory and practice; rather, the reformers are concentrating on establishing methods for connecting the two.

This book is designed to permit linkages between acquired knowledge and the world of practice. Case studies have been shown to be a powerful teaching tool in the preparation of professional practitioners. This has been especially true with business executives, physicians, and attorneys.

My interest in case studies evolved through the 1980s. After making an abrupt career shift from being a school superintendent to a professor of school administration at a research university, I came to realize how critical it was to bridge the theories I taught in the classroom with the real-world experiences I acquired as a practitioner. Increasingly, I infused vignettes into my teaching to provide examples of how theory could be used. The vignettes gradually became longer until they were abandoned in favor of case studies. My students responded enthusiastically to the teaching paradigm.

The case method of teaching permits you to be an active learner. You are able to examine how myriad variables affect your decisions as a leader. Most importantly, you learn that technical knowledge without problem-solving skills and reflective thinking is of limited value in the real world.

During my career, I have been privileged to work with many individuals who, by example, taught me the value of bridging theory with practice. Professors James Rentschler and Alex Moody of Indiana State University, Professor Howard Smucker of Loyola University in Chicago, Professor Everett Nicholson of Purdue University, and Professors Michael Grady and Gerard Fowler of Saint Louis University are educators who believe that school administrators must be adept at implementing the knowledge they acquire in professional school. I am indebted to them for their ideas and insights.

A special note of appreciation is extended to the superintendents, principals, and other practitioners who assisted in the preparation of the cases in this book. Dr. Michael Benway and Dr. Phillip McDaniel are two superintendents who were especially helpful in providing critical analysis. Additionally, Steve Dickerson, my doctoral fellow, Diane Meyer, and Tamara Peach of Ball State University were extremely helpful in preparing the manuscript. Finally, I thank my wife, Mary Anne, and children, Catherine, Christopher, Timothy, and Thomas, for always being supportive.

CASE STUDIES ON
EDUCATIONAL
ADMINISTRATION

Introduction

In the varied topography of professional practice, there is a high hard ground overlooking the swamp. On the high ground, manageable problems lend themselves to solutions through the application of research-based theory and technique. In the swampy lowland, messy, confusing problems defy technical solution.

—*Donald Schon*

Most graduate programs in school administration are designed to prepare practitioners. True, there are a few curricula at research institutions that focus on research and teaching roles in higher education; but the vast majority of universities offering graduate degrees in educational leadership are engaged in the preservice and continuing education of principals, central office personnel (directors and assistant superintendents), and superintendents. Historically, graduate programs in departments of educational administration have been occupied with the transmission of technical skills. In the past twenty-five to thirty years, the complexity of practice has led a number of administrators to complain that their academic programs simply did not prepare them well in certain key areas, for example, human relations (Brookhart, 1987). These same criticisms have come more recently from national reform panels.

Institutions have responded in varying ways to the environmental and professional pressures to reform. Some analysts have attributed the lack of relevance in administrator preparation to an overemphasis on theory; others (e.g., National Policy Board for Educational Administration, 1989) have called for a national reformation that would install a radically different curriculum for graduate study in

1

school administration; and still others have simply concluded that the programs are adequate as they now exist. The alternatives of doing nothing and of lowering the emphasis on theory and the behavioral sciences are especially troublesome judgments. In reality, the deemphasis of theory increases, de facto, the attention devoted to teaching technical skills.

Professors of educational administration often disagree on the most important elements of advanced graduate study in school administration and how those elements are best delivered. Even deans of education, for instance, differ markedly on such functional requirements as the doctoral residency (Kowalski, 1989/90). If educational administration is to be a respected profession, then graduate study must require no less rigor in leadership than is required for other professional degrees.

In truth, the issue is not one of theory versus technical skills. Rather, the effective preparation of practitioners entails melding the two. As Schon (1983) aptly noted, many practitioners in contemporary society are bewildered because technical skills alone are no longer sufficient for effective practice. All professions and all practitioners are affected by the dynamics of the general environment; and as such, the mere possession of technical knowledge is not sufficient. For example, the technical skills learned by physicians twenty years ago in medical school are of limited value today unless they are able to integrate those skills with technology and advances in medicine, and to apply this knowledge within the context of today's political, social, and economic realities. To do this physicians must not only keep current but must also be capable of reflective practice.

Schon (1983) noted:

> The study of reflection-in-action is critically important. The dilemma of rigor or relevance may be dissolved if we can develop an epistemology of practice which places technical problem solving within a broader context of reflective inquiry, shows how reflection-in-action may be rigorous in its own right. (p. 69)

The practitioner needs opportunities to apply acquired knowledge prior to entering practice and to learn how to reflect the meaning of these clinical activities. Writing about needs in teacher education, Doyle (1985) observed:

> For clinical experience to be fruitful in developing appropriate knowledge structures, however, beginning teachers must receive descriptive, analytical feedback about performance. In other words, the clinical program must include experience and an opportunity to reflect upon the meaning of the experience. (p. 33)

The practitioner in educational administration should be thoroughly practiced in theoretical reflection, philosophical inquiry, research, and history, as well as prepared in the areas of administrative and technical practice. The graduate experience should emphasize the theoretical dimensions of practice, the historical roots of school administration practice, and research instead of the simple transmission of techniques. One of the most essential tasks for professors of educational leadership is the effective bridging of theories with established craft knowledge. To do this, professors must devote more attention to the application of knowledge, and students must be prepared to incorporate reflection into their knowledge practices.

Case Studies on Educational Administration focuses on one proven method of associating academic study with the real world of school administration—the case study. Educational reform reports in the 1980s accurately cited the need for the infusion of reality into preparation programs for educators (e.g., Task Force on Teaching as a Profession, 1986). As noted, these recommendations are not novel; they reinforce what studies of practitioners already indicated. In an interview regarding needed improvements in the preparation of professional educators, Lee Shulman stated it this way:

> I'd like to see much greater use of cases, much like what is done in law and business education. That might reorient the teaching of teachers from the current model, which is either entirely field based, where you have little control over what goes on, or entirely classroom based, where everything is artificial. We have to create a middle ground, where problems of theory and practice can intersect in a realistic way. The genius of the case method, especially in business, is that you use realistic problems, but you can still deal with both the theoretical and the tactical aspects. (Brandt, 1988, p. 43)

DEFINING CASE STUDIES

A case is a description of an administrative situation, commonly involving a decision or problem (Erskine, Leenders, & Mauffette-Leenders, 1981). Frequently, the terms *case study* and *case method* are used interchangeably. This is an error. A case study is the general description of a situation and may have several purposes: (1) as a method of research, (2) as a method of evaluation, (3) as a method of policy studies, and (4) as a teaching method. Thus, case study refers to the narrative description of the incident, not its intended purpose. *Case method,* on the other hand, has specific reference to using the case studies as a teaching paradigm. More specifically, the case method entails a technique whereby the major ingredients of a case study are presented to students for the purpose of studying behaviors or problem-solving techniques.

There are several other related terms that may cause confusion and, thus, deserve explanation. One of these is *case work.* This term is commonly used in psychology, sociology, social work, and medicine. It connotes the development, adjustment, remedial, or corrective procedures that appropriately follow diagnosis of the causes of maladjustment. Another term is *case history.* This refers to tracing a person, group, or organization's past (Merriam, 1988). Being able to distinguish all of these terms facilitates the effective use of the professional literature on the topic of case studies.

THE CASE METHOD AS AN INSTRUCTIONAL PARADIGM

Essentially, case studies can serve two purposes when used as a teaching model. First, they can be employed to teach new information, concepts, and theories. For example, the professor may attempt to teach that conflict in organizations is inevitable and then ask you to deal with new knowledge through the process of induction. That is, by reading a case that exemplifies the concept, you will hopefully note associations between certain factors. When these associations are repeated (e.g., in other cases), you are expected to master the concept through induction. In addition, the cases can be used as a vehicle for applying acquired knowledge and skills in specific situations. Application can serve several goals such as teaching reasoning, critical thinking, and problem-solving skills. In this respect, application also can be used to teach concepts (e.g., general problem solving) as well as skills, but the concepts are related to processes associated with leadership and management.

There are two universal aspects of the case method. One is the Socratic Method and the other is the presentation of selected information (e.g., facts about individuals, facts about school districts). This information is referred to as *situational knowledge*. Each person who reads a case is exposed to the same situational knowledge. Why then do these individuals often differ in their interpretations of the case? The information obtained from the case is processed by the individual. This processing is called abstraction. Individuals essentially filter situational knowledge through their values, beliefs, experiences, and acquired knowledge. Because we do not share identical philosophies, experiences, and education, and because we do not possess equal levels of ability with regard to processing information, we tend to arrive at different outputs when we abstract information. In studying the ways in which teachers make decisions, Shavelson and Stern (1981) observed the following:

> People selectively perceive and interpret portions of available information with respect to their goals, and construct a simplified model of reality. Using certain heuristics, attributions and other psychological mechanisms, people then make judgements and decisions that carry them out on the basis of their psychological model of reality. (p. 461)

These outputs become critical in experiencing the case method. They explain why individuals, even experienced practitioners, do not have identical reactions to situational knowledge. These outputs in the case method are referred to as *specific knowledge*. The practitioner formulates a response or course of action based on specific knowledge.

PREVALENT USES OF CASE STUDIES IN EDUCATION

Within schools of education, case studies have been used more frequently as a research tool than as an instructional strategy. The growing acceptance of qualitative research in the social sciences has magnified the value of case studies. Ethnographic research is the best known of the qualitative techniques. The work of Yin (1984) is especially enlightening for individuals wishing to explore the use of case studies as a research methodology. He noted that case studies are used for research in many settings including policy analysis, public administration, community psychology and sociology, organization and management studies, and public service agencies. More recently, ethnography has been encouraged as a method for better understanding the work environment of professional educators (e.g., Erickson, 1986).

Many schools of education house departments in educational and counseling psychology. In these units, case histories and case work are infused into academic study and clinical experiences. But beyond qualitative research and practice in psychology, the case study has not been a conspicuous component of graduate work in education. That is not to say that experimentation with the approach has not occurred in educational administration. Some similar techniques aimed at bridging theory and practice, such as simulations and "in-basket" programs, have been periodically attempted. In the mid-1950s, several texts were published on case studies (e.g., Hamburg, 1955; Sargent & Belisle, 1955), but the procedure never really became a standard component of the curricula for the preparation of educational leaders. Rather, the use of cases has largely depended on the initiatives and interests of individual professors. It should be noted that the University Council for Educational Administration (UCEA) and leaders in that group have advocated the use of case studies and simulations for over three decades (e.g., Culbertson & Coffield, 1960; Griffiths, 1963). Recent research verifies that practitioners continue to identify the lecture method of teaching as the most common instructional technique they encountered in graduate school (Witters-Churchill, 1988).

Clark (1986) contended that because of the complexity of educational administration, multiple approaches ought to be used in preservice and inservice education. She noted that the traditional management approach is suitable for teaching specific tasks; but, an emphasis on information gathering, observation skills, and analytical skills is best served by other teaching paradigms designed to engage the learner more fully in the classroom activities. Despite such recognition, case studies have not been widely incorporated into the formal education programs for educational leaders.

SIMULATION AS A TEACHING TOOL

Professional schools rely on several methods to expose students to the real world of practice. Internship is one of the most common approaches. This segment of the curriculum is typically structured as a capstone experience; and although valuable, it does not provide early and continuous experiences permitting the graduate student to associate theory with practice. Recognizing this limitation, many professors of educational leadership are expressing an interest in alternative teaching strategies that will permit a greater infusion of reality into all course work. Studies in teacher education, for example, exhibit that linkages between clinical experiences and methods classes provide an improved format for teaching.

Simulation is designed to create vicarious experiences for the students—an approximation of the practitioner's challenges, problems, opportunities, and so forth. It is a form of teaching that can be used at all stages of a graduate program. There are two general approaches to using simulation as a teaching paradigm: (1) providing complete data about a given situation before requiring the student to address the problem, and (2) providing basic information sufficient to permit the student to address the problem. The former approach is best characterized by in-basket techniques. In this process, the student is given detailed information about a position, problem, and so forth. Often this requires the student to spend a great deal of time studying the documents (e.g., budgets, memoranda). This approach is often used when specific problem-solving skills are addressed. The latter approach focuses on using the essential information of a given situation. This information is most often transmitted in the form of a case study. This option is usually employed when general problem-solving skills are addressed.

Many educators continue to believe that simulation can only be successful if extensive supporting data are used to provide the student a sufficient information base. This notion is rejected in this book. Simulations using what Cunningham (1971) called a *non-material based approach* were proven to be successful when used with educators at the University of Chicago in the mid-1960s. In fact, Cunningham noted that he changed his own views about the necessity of detailed information after viewing the successes with simulation under these conditions.

USING THEORY TO MAKE DECISIONS

There are many misconceptions about theory. Some view it as a dream representing the wishes of an individual or group. Others perceive theory to be a supposition or speculation or a philosophy (Owens, 1981). In reality theories are used to synthesize, organize, and classify facts that emerge from observations and data collections in varying situations (e.g., research studies). They are developed by interfacing data collected on the same variables as they exist in different situations and/or environments. Hoy and Miskel (1987) characterized theories in educational administration as interrelated concepts, assumptions, and generalizations that systematically describe and explain regularities in behavior.

Educational leaders have the same decision options available to all other types of administrators and managers. When confronted with circumstances demanding action, the individual may choose one of several behaviors:

1. ignore the situation and refuse to make a decision
2. make a decision on the basis of instinct
3. get someone else to make the decision
4. imitate the perceived successful behavior of other practitioners
5. make a decision on the basis of accumulated information which creates the likelihood that the response you choose will be effective (Kowalski, 1988)

Any of the first four alternatives may provide a short-term solution, but continual reliance on these options is apt to eventually create problems. The final option exhibits the choice of an educated leader. It entails the utilization of information as well as academic and craft knowledge to create alternative decisions (contingencies), the weighing of these alternatives, and, given the prevailing conditions, the selection of the most suitable option. Often theory alone is insufficient. The practitioner needs to develop problem-solving skills that permit the appropriate application of knowledge.

Among the numerous decision-making models used in administration, the best known and most widely used is probably the *rational-analytical model*. This paradigm consists of four steps: (1) defining the problem, (2) diagnosing the problem, (3) searching for alternative solutions, and (4) evaluating alternative solutions. Case studies are an excellent vehicle for applying this and similar decision-making models. Students can complete all four stages of the rational-analytical model by reading and reacting to the cases.

The cases presented in this book may be addressed using any of the decision alternatives cited here. However, it is expected that you will apply accumulated knowledge and theory to the situations being analyzed. This processing results in specific knowledge that provides the framework for your administrative behavior.

Is decision making a science, or is it an art? Clearly, leaders who master the use of decision-making models are less prone to errors than those administrators who try to make key decisions solely on the basis of instinct. There is an advantage with the rational-analytical approach because it permits the leader to apply general problem-solving skills to specific situations. Developing the knowledge and skill necessary to do this is one purpose of using case studies. Each case provides a novel set of variables affecting the choices available to an administrator. The community, the school district, the challenge, and the individual personalities are examples of variables that must be considered in reaching decisions. When practitioners rely on theories to analyze the existing conditions under which a choice must be made, they are using a scientific approach to decision making. This technique is strengthened through practice as the individual leader amalgamates theoretical knowledge with craft knowledge. The practitioner is expected to become increasingly skillful in applying general problem-solving abilities to specific situations.

The evolution of literature on the topic of decision making exhibits the movement of graduate study in educational leadership from a narrow training focus on technical skills to one where behavioral studies now play a critical role. In concluding that accumulated information about decision processes were eradicating the comfort of simple solutions, Estler (1988) wrote:

> We might replace recipes with skills in analysis of organizational dynamics and contexts. Though the ambiguities of educational decision-making cannot be eliminated, they can be made more understandable and less threatening. By understanding a variety of approaches to decision-making and the range of organizational conditions under which they may be applicable, the administrator can be better prepared to respond to, and even enjoy, organizational ambiguity and complexity. (p. 316)

More than any other element of graduate study in educational administration, it is the knowledge base relative to decision making that illuminates the value of infusing case studies into graduate education. Those who still contend that there are tried and true recipes for leadership behavior that work in all situations under all sorts of conditions are either misguided or uninformed.

THE CONTENT OF THIS BOOK

This book contains twenty-five cases that were selected to exemplify the diversity of challenges in contemporary educational leadership. You should not look at any case as having a single dimension even though the title or primary focus of the material may lead you to that conclusion. Actually the cases are quite intricate with multiple foci—exactly the way problems exist in the real world of practice. For example, a single case may involve conflict resolution, effective communication, power, and leadership style.

There are three types of case studies: (1) true cases, (2) disguised cases, and (3) fictitious cases (Matejka & Cosse, 1981). True cases are presented with absolutely no data changes; that is, names, places, dates remain intact. Disguised cases are descriptions of real situations, but the names of actors, locations, organizations, and the like are altered to assure anonymity. Fictitious cases (also referred to as *armchair cases)* are hypothetical examples to illustrate a principle, concept, or specific set of conditions. The cases presented in this book are disguised incidents. Each is based on a situation that occurred in the past fifteen years. The real names of individuals, school districts, schools, and communities have been changed. Often when these cases are presented in workshops, someone will say, "I know that situation; I know where this case occurred." This response is common because the challenges presented in these cases recur in the practice of school administration.

The cases are erected around six basic themes:

- The Work Environment of Educational Leaders
- Making Decisions
- Human Relations and Communication
- Resolving Conflict
- Instructional Leadership
- Policy, Politics, and Other Emerging Issues

The themes were used merely to try to balance the content of the cases in the book. As mentioned previously, the cases have multiple foci and some cases could relate to three or four of the themes.

The narrative format for individual cases is not uniform. Some are divided into sections with information about the community, school district, school, and the incident presented under subheadings. Other cases do not have these subheadings. Although it would be convenient to follow a standard format, the student of educational administration must recognize that information in the real world of practice does not come in standardized packages. The variance in the way information is presented in the cases reflects the unevenness of communication in school districts and schools. Indeed, one of the skills that educational leaders need to develop is the ability to use information presented in different forms.

One of the goals of the case method is to have the students become proficient at filtering information. The practitioner needs to learn to separate the important and relevant facts from those data that have little or no bearing on the decision. This is especially important in simulation activities. Thus, one should not assume that all the information presented in a case is critical. Your responses to the cases, and in effect your leadership behavior, will depend on the information you determine to be important.

Although the narratives vary, the format for presenting the material following the description of each case is uniform. At this point three components are introduced:

1. a Challenge
2. Key Issues and Questions
3. Suggested Readings

In a classroom setting, the instructor determines how these supplemental components will be utilized in conjunction with the case.

Case studies vary markedly in structure and length because they are used for different purposes. Some may be only a few paragraphs long, whereas others span hundreds of pages (Immegart, 1971). This point is important because some continue to believe that all case studies must conform to a set of prescribed data standards. The cases in this book are purposefully not taken to their conclusion in order that simulations and situational teaching can be used in conjunction with the cases.

EFFECTIVELY ENGAGING IN THE CASE METHOD

Two extremely important factors have already been mentioned regarding the effective use of cases. First, information filtering permits the reader to isolate the pertinent data that are needed for making a decision. Second, using accumulated information and knowledge in a systematic fashion, (i.e., utilizing a decision-making model) produces more enlightened decisions. With regard to this latter point, it is important to recognize the difference between education and training. Educated persons rely on past experiences and knowledge to make behavioral choices. Training, by contrast, focuses on a prescribed response given specific conditions (e.g., repairing a television). The concept of reflective thinking is essential for professional development and constitutes one of the distinguishing features of professional practice. In this respect, each day becomes a learning experience for the practitioner.

Frequently, educational leaders are puzzled by situations where the same response to a given problem produces vastly different results. Take, for example, a specific approach to discipline. Why would a method work very well in one school and be a disaster in another? The answer rests largely with organizational and environmental variables. If the administrator ignores the conditions under which a decision must be made, the probability of error markedly increases. Put simply, decision-making processes in educational organizations are affected by existing conditions (Estler, 1988).

Beyond information filtering and the recognition of what constitutes an educated response, it is critical to note that the case method does not seek the "one right answer." Romm and Mahler (1986) noted that this is particularly true when the cases are used in conjunction with the rational-analytical model for making decisions:

> Basing the analysis of the case on the rational-analytical decision making model, implicitly carries the message that there are no "right" or "wrong" solutions to the case. By applying the model to cases, students realize that a case always has many problems, and the definition of one of these problems as the "main" problem is often subjective and arbitrary. They also realize that once a problem has been defined, it can have different meanings and be solved in different ways, depending on whose interests are being served or being given priority. (p. 695)

One of the valuable experiences of working with case studies entails the analysis of a multitude of potential behaviors. Cases provide an open invitation to generalize (Biddle & Anderson, 1986). Thus, creativity and imagination are encouraged. When the cases are discussed in group settings (e.g., the classroom), the individual can benefit from both self-analysis and the analysis of peer behavior.

The case method differs significantly from the lecture method of teaching. It is designed to allow you to apply technical skills, concepts, and craft knowledge in the context of unique circumstances, and to develop reflective thinking and problem-solving skills at the same time.

Although the educated person is expected to rely on accumulated experiences and knowledge to formulate decisions, a person's behavior is never void of personal values and beliefs. This reality makes the case method even more challenging and exciting. Two graduate students sharing common educational experiences may arrive at two divergent positions for a given case. Why? As noted earlier, each person develops specific knowledge through a process of abstraction. In selecting leadership responses, you rely on more than experience. Your values, beliefs, knowledge, and problem-solving skills all contribute to your own world of reality at the psychological level.

There is one additional dimension of the case method that is undervalued. You will work with these cases in a social context. That is, you will interact with other students in making decisions and reflecting on the decisions of others. The presence of others in the case method context approximates the real world. Superintendents and principals do not make decisions in isolation. Their behavior is constantly evaluated by those in their work and community environments. In this respect, the social context of learning is enhanced via the case method because it permits the pursuit of both affective and cognitive domain goals.

SOME FINAL SUGGESTIONS

Engaging in case studies in a group setting requires several caveats regarding personal behavior. First, the process is an active one. Simulation carried out in a classroom environment is a form of cooperative learning. It offers an opportunity to be candid and to learn from both positive and negative decisions. It permits every participant to be a learner and a transmitter of knowledge. In addition, it is essential that the participants exhibit mutual respect. Keep in mind that analysis is most meaningful when open dialogue is possible. Disagreements are inevitable in this instructional format. The institutional purpose is not to declare one person right and the other wrong; rather, the process seeks to bridge experience, knowledge, and personal values and beliefs with practice to create a better understanding of leadership behavior.

The observations made with the case method provide a useful resource for practice. Thus, the development of a notebook in conjunction with classroom experiences is highly advised. Although no two situations are ever identical, the general principles addressed in the twenty-five cases are likely to recur throughout one's tenure as an educational leader.

REFERENCES

Biddle, B., & Anderson, D. (1986). Theory, methods, knowledge, and research on teaching. In M. Wittrock (Ed.), *Handbook of research on teaching* (3rd ed.), pp. 230–252. New York: Macmillan.

Brandt, R. (1988). An assessment of teaching: A conversation with Lee Shulman. *Educational Leadership, 46*(3), 42–47.

Brookhart, L. (1987). *Comparisons of professor, student, and principal perceptions of preparation programs for educational leaders.* Unpublished Ph.D. thesis, University of Denver.

Christensen, C. (1987). *Teaching and the case method.* Boston: Harvard Business School.

Clark, V. (1986). The effectiveness of case studies in training principals. Using the deliberative orientation. *Peabody Journal of Education, 63,* 187–195.

Culbertson, J., & Coffield, W. (Eds.) (1960). *Simulation in administration training.* Columbus, OH: University Council for Educational Administration.

Cunningham, L. (1971). A powerul but underdeveloped educational tool. In D. Bolton (Ed.), *The use of simulation in educational administration,* pp. 1–29. Columbus, OH: Charles E. Merrill.

Doyle, W. (1985). Recent research on classroom management: Implications for teacher preparation. *Journal of Teacher Education, 36,* 31–35.

Erickson, F. (1986). Qualitative methods in research on teaching. In M. Wittrock (Ed.), *Handbook of research on teaching* (3rd ed.), pp. 119–161. New York: Macmillan.

Erskine, J., Leenders, M., & Mauffette-Leenders, L. (1981). *Teaching with cases.* London, Canada: School of Business Administration, University of Western Ontario.

Estler, S. (1988). *Decision making.* In N. Boyan (Ed.), *Handbook of research on educational administration,* pp. 305–350. White Plains, NY: Longman.

Griffith, D. (1963). The case method of teaching educational administration: A re-appraisal, 1963. *Journal of Educational Administration, 1*(2), 81–82.

Hamburg, M. (1955). *Case studies in elementary school administration.* New York: Bureau of Publications, Teachers College, Columbia University.

Hoy, C., & Miskel, C. (1987). *Education administration* (3rd ed.). New York: Random House.

Immegart, G. (1971). The use of cases. In D. Bolton (Ed.), *The use of simulation in educational administration,* pp. 30–64. Columbus, OH: Charles E. Merrill.

Kowalski, T. (1988). *The organization and planning of adult education.* Albany, NY: State University of New York Press.

Kowalski, T. (1989/90). Perspectives of deans of education on educational administration. *National Forum of Educational Administration and Supervision Journal, 7*(1), 104–116.

Kowalski, T., Weaver, R., & Henson, K. (1990). *Case studies on teaching.* White Plains, NY: Longman.

Matejka, J., & Cosse, T. (1981). *The business case method: An introduction.* Richmond, VA: Robert F. Dame.

Merriam, S. (1988). *Case research in education.* San Francisco: Jossey-Bass.

National Policy Board for Educational Administration (1989). *Improving the preparation of school administrators: An agenda for reform.* Charlottesville, VA: Author.

Owens, R. (1981). *Organizational behavior in education* (2nd ed.). Englewood Cliffs, NJ: Prentice-Hall.

Romm, T., & Mahler, S. (1986). A three dimensional model for using case studies in the academic classroom. *Higher Education, 15,* 677–696.

Sargent, C., & Belisle, E. (1955). *Educational administration: Cases and concepts.* Boston: Houghton-Mifflin.

Schon, D. (1983). *The reflective practitioner.* New York: Basic Books.

Schon, D. (1990). *Educating the reflective practitioner,* p. 3. San Francisco: Jossey-Bass.

Shavelson, R., & Stern, P. (1981). Research on teachers pedagogical thoughts, judgements, decisions, and behavior. *Review of Educational Research, 51,* 455–498.

Task Force on Teaching as a Profession (1986). *A nation prepared: Teachers for the 21st century.* New York: Carnegie Forum.

Witters-Churchill, L. (1988). *University preparation of the school administrator: Evaluations by Texas principals.* Unpublished Ph.D. thesis, Texas A & M University.

Yin, R. (1984). *Case study research.* Beverly Hills, CA: Sage Publications.

CASE 1

The Principal Changes Some Valued Rules

Oliver Wendell Holmes Elementary School is the third oldest facility in this far-western major city. It is located in a neighborhood that has substantially deteriorated in the past three decades. The drab brick exterior and rectangular shape are constant reminders of the unimaginative nature of school facility design in the 1940s. The cracked sidewalks are soiled with endless works of graffiti, written in English and Spanish and displaying every color of the rainbow. The playground is covered with weeds and litter and the broken swings and teeter-totters attest to the fact that school officials no longer attempt to keep the area functional.

John Lattimore has been principal of Holmes Elementary School for the past three years. He is a veteran administrator, having served at three other elementary schools in the district prior to this assignment. In total, he has been an educator for thirty-one years, twenty-two as a principal. When the vacancy occurred at Holmes, John was the only sitting principal in the district who applied for the position. Several of his peers on the district's administrative staff thought he had lost his mind for doing so. John had a school in one of the city's better neighborhoods. Why would he want to return to the social and economic problems that permeated the areas immediately surrounding the core of the city? In his interview with the superintendent and assistant superintendent for elementary education, John simply said he wanted a change of scenery. For those who knew John, it was a believable answer.

Given that experienced administrators were not standing in line to become the principal at Holmes Elementary, Dr. Gray, the superintendent, was only too happy to oblige Mr. Lattimore. Having a seasoned administrator take the assignment was a pleasant surprise for the central office administrators. Typically, such difficult and undesirable assignments are given to individuals seeking their first principalship (a practice that has always puzzled observers).

The three years at Holmes Elementary School seemed to pass very quickly for John. The first year was essentially an adjustment period. He tried to meet most of the parents, learn every child's name, and develop a positive working relationship with the faculty. The second year was marked by substantial changes in rules and regulations. In particular, John tried to: (1) revamp the school's discipline program, one that heavily relied on corporal punishment and suspensions; and (2) alter the practice of failing a significant number of students. The third year evolved into a quagmire of conflict. A significant number of teachers and parents voiced strong objections to what they perceived as an unduly liberal approach to the management of student conduct and enforcement of academic standards.

The dissatisfaction with Mr. Lattimore was pervasive. A parent's group was demanding that he be transferred to another school. Slightly over one-half of faculty agreed with this suggestion and signed a letter of no confidence that was forwarded to the assistant superintendent for elementary education.

In making changes in rules and regulations, John's approach was to present his concerns and intentions in faculty meetings. The information was transmitted to the teachers in the form of announcements—discussion regarding the principal's initiatives was not encouraged. Mr. Lattimore told teachers to see him individually if they wished to discuss the operational changes he was instituting. Fearing one-to-one communications with the principal, most teachers did not exercise this option. Informal communication via the "grapevine" in the school indicated that a number of teachers did not trust the principal. Although John knew there was some dissatisfaction with his leadership style, he underestimated the intensity of the discontentment. His eyes were opened, however, when he received a copy of the "no confidence" letter that had been sent to Dr. Jeanelle Danton, the assistant superintendent for elementary education and his immediate supervisor.

Dear Dr. Danton:

Undoubtedly you receive many complaints from teachers who disagree with their principals. Please do not consider this letter to be one of those routine grievances. Over the past two and one-half years, the teachers at Oliver Wendell Holmes Elementary School have observed the leadership capabilities of Mr. John Lattimore. While he is a friendly, industrious, and intelligent person, his approach to dealing with the children at school simply is ineffective.

Most of the children who attend this school come from one-parent families living below the poverty level. Many receive little or no direction with regard to their personal behavior outside of school. Even the parents and guardians of the students recognize that the school must be a major force in providing discipline for the children. Since arriving at our school, Mr. Lattimore has gradually changed all of the established regulations related to discipline. He has made it impossible to administer corporal punishment or to utilize suspensions. He encourages social promotions. Although we do not dispute his judgment that these children lack love and understanding, we reject his belief that the school can be the parent, the psychologist, the social worker, and the friend that each troubled child needs. Allowing disruptive children to remain in school deprives other children of their opportunities to learn.

It is with heavy hearts that we must notify you that we have no confidence in Mr. John Lattimore to be principal of Oliver Wendell Holmes Elementary School. Perhaps his talents can be utilized more productively in another assignment. He is a good person who means well. He cannot, however, effectively lead this school. We ask that he be removed as principal as soon as possible.

Respectfully,

(signed by 18 of the 26 teachers)

The school district has eighty-seven elementary schools, most located in inner-city neighborhoods. Although complaints about principals are not uncommon, a letter of no confidence signed by most of the teachers at a school is another matter. A copy of the letter was sent to the union president. This fact always adds another dimension to the problem. Immediately on receiving the letter, Dr. Danton telephoned Lattimore and arranged an appointment to discuss the teachers' claims. The two administrators met the following day in the central offices of the school district.

John Lattimore opened the discussion by candidly stating that he was shocked when he received his copy of the letter. He also noted his anger regarding the discourtesy he felt his faculty displayed in sending the letter without first notifying him of their intentions.

"You mean you had no idea there was this level of concern among your staff members?" inquired his supervisor.

"Well," John responded, "Several of the teachers voiced displeasure with my changing some of the rules and regulations related to discipline. You know, Jeanelle, you were a principal. Teachers don't always agree with you. Everyone is entitled to an opinion. Unfortunately, someone has to be in charge; someone has to make the difficult decisions. No, I knew there was some displeasure; I just didn't think it was so widespread."

John Lattimore and Jeanelle Danton were old friends. They served as fellow elementary principals and John wrote a letter of support when she applied for her current position. Their professional relationship was marked by mutual respect as well as friendship. This relationship made the meeting more difficult for both of them.

"John, didn't you know how strong these feelings were among the teachers? Didn't you discuss the rules and regulations with them before you made changes?" Dr. Danton inquired.

"The changes were discussed. We never voted on them, but they were discussed. I thought most of the teachers were willing to give a different approach a chance. Listen, I've been around these children for a long time—and so have you. Their lives are filled with grief and disappointments. Why should school become another enemy, just another miserable experience? Maybe, just maybe, by showing some love and compassion for these children we could turn a few lives around. Maybe we could convince a few children that someone cares. Isn't that important? What do we accomplish when we suspend a child from school? We're punishing the parent, not the child. How will we ever teach these children to be responsible for their own behavior if we constantly impose negative reinforcements on them?"

"What about this issue of social promotions?" asked the assistant superintendent.

"Failing children who are already at-risk simply does not work. They prefer to say that I favor social promotions. I prefer to say that I condemn failing children when it just makes it more likely they will be unsuccessful."

Dr. Danton looked directly at him and asked, "John, would you consider taking another assignment at this time? I can arrange for you to work with me here in the central office. I need a director of pupil personnel services. It would mean an increase in salary and it would be a good way to resolve this problem. Now I don't want you to think that I'm trying to get you out of the school. I really would like to have you here working with me in the central office. Lord knows, you've earned it. You have put in your time in the trenches. What do you think?"

"Jeanelle, you know the answer. I've had other opportunities to work here in the central office. That's not my cup of tea. I want to be with the kids. No, I'm sorry. I'm not going to run away from this. I think I am right and if you give me the time, I think I can turn the parents and teachers around. Why is everyone so sure that my changes won't be successful? I thought the principal was supposed to be the leader. All I'm asking for is the opportunity to do my job."

As the principal left her office, Dr. Danton remembered that Mr. Lattimore also belonged to a union. The principals' union in the school district was every bit as strong as the teachers' union. She wished that her friend had been more compromising and accepted her offer.

THE CHALLENGE: Place yourself in the position of Dr. Danton. What would you do at this point?

KEY ISSUES/QUESTIONS:

1. Identify the range of options available to the assistant superintendent in this matter.
2. If you were the principal and wanted to change rules and regulations regarding discipline, would you have required consensus from the teachers to do so?
3. Do you believe it was proper for Dr. Danton to offer the principal a job in central administration to resolve the issue? Why or why not?
4. Is the principal correct in his judgment that corporal punishment and suspensions provide negative reinforcement that deters the development of self-discipline?
5. Discuss the rights of the troubled child in relation to classmates. Are the teachers correct in their contention that permitting a disruptive child to remain in the classroom deprives other students of their opportunity to learn?
6. What weight should be given to the fact that many parents are also unhappy with the principal's positions on discipline?
7. What information is not provided in this case that you consider important to reaching a decision?

8. Identify the advantages and disadvantages of Dr. Danton following the recommendation of the disgruntled teachers to remove Mr. Lattimore as principal.

9. What can be assumed about the teachers who did not sign the letter of no confidence?

10. Can you suggest any positive action that might bring the parents, teachers, and principal together to address this problem?

11. Does failing children increase the likelihood that they will be unsuccessful in school?

SUGGESTED READINGS:

Alson, A., et al. (1983). Shaping a plan for school improvement: Alternative approaches. *Journal of Staff Development, 4*(1), 25–42.

Auer, M., & Nisenholz, B. (1987). Humanistic processes and bureaucratic structures—Are they compatible? *NASSP Bulletin, 71*(495), 96–101.

Blase, J. (1984). Teacher coping and school principal behaviors. *Contemporary Education, 56*(1), 21–25.

Blase, J. (1985). The phenomenology of teacher stress: Implications for organizational theory and research. *Administrator's Notebook, 31*(7), 1–4.

Bridgeland, W., & Duane, E. (1987). Elementary school principals and their political settings. *Urban Review, 19*(4), 191–200.

Burke, T. (1987). *Teacher participation in decision-making.* Unpublished Psy. D. thesis, Rutgers, State University of New Jersey.

Carey, M. (1986). School discipline: Better to be loved or feared? *Momentum, 17*(2), 20–21.

Crooker, R., & Brooker, G. (1986). Classroom control and student outcomes in grades 2 and 5. *American Educational Research Journal, 23*(1), 1–11.

Curwin, R., & Mendler, A. (1988). Packaged discipline programs: Let the buyer beware. *Educational Leadership, 46*(6), 68–71.

Docking, R. (1985). Changing teacher pupil control ideology and teacher anxiety. *Journal of Education for Teaching, 11*(1), 63–76.

Drake, T., & Roe, W. (1986). *The principalship* (3rd ed.), chap. 16. New York: Macmillan.

Erickson, H. (1988). The boy who couldn't be disciplined. *Principal, 67*(5), 36–37.

Fine, M., & Holt, P. (1983). Corporal punishment in the family: A systems perspective. *Psychology in the Schools, 20*(1), 85–92.

Gottredson, D. (1987). An evaluation of an organizational development approach to reducing school disorders. *Evaluation Review, 11*(6), 739–763.

Guthrie, J., & Reed, R. (1986). *Educational administration and policy,* pp. 325–344. Englewood Cliffs, NJ: Prentice-Hall.

Johnston, G., & Venable, B. (1986). A study of teacher loyalty to the principal: Rule administration and hierarchical influence of the principal. *Educational Administration Quarterly, 22*(4), 4–27.

Laughter, K. (1988). Nothing was ever Timothy's fault. *Learning, 16*(9), 38–40.

Lowe, R., & Gervais, R. (1984). Tackling a problem school. *Principal, 63*(5), 8–12.

Lunenburg, F. (1987). Another face of school climate. *Illinois Student Journal, 67*(1), 3–10.

Lutz, J., et al. (1987). The Caloosa School: A model for success. *Principal, 66*(4), 18–20.

Maynard, B. (1983). Is your discipline policy part of your discipline problem? *Executive Educator, 5*(3), 26–27.

McDaniel, T. (1986). School discipline in perspective. *Clearing House, 59*(8), 369–370.

Menacker, J. (1988). Legislating school discipline: The application of a systemwide discipline code for schools in a large urban district. *Urban Education, 23*(1), 12–23.

Menaker, J., Weldon, W., & Hurwitz, E. (1989). School order and safety as community issues. *Phi Delta Kappan, 71*(1), 39–40, 55–56.

Moore, W., & Cooper, H. (1984). Correlations between teacher and student background and teacher perceptions of discipline problems and disciplinary techniques. *Psychology in the Schools, 21*(3), 386–392.

Ornstein, A. (1982). Student disruptions and student rights: An overview. *Urban Education, 14*(2), 83–91.

Reitman, A. (1988). Corporal punishment in schools—The ultimate violence. *Children's Legal Rights Journal, 9*(33), 6–13.

Slavin, R., & Madden, N. (1989). What works for students at-risk: A research synthesis. *Educational Leadership, 46*(5), 4–13.

Snyder, K., & Anderson, R. (1986). *Managing productive schools: Toward an ecology,* pp. 111–123. Orlando, FL: Academic Press College Division.

Thomas, W. (1988). To solve "the discipline problem," mix clear rules with consistent consequences. *American School Board Journal, 175*(6), 30–31.

Vasiloff, B. (1983). The teacher's vital role in developing student discipline. *Momentum, 13*(4), 23–26.

Wynne, E. (1986). Character development: Renewing an old commitment. *Principal, 65*(3), 28–31.

Wynne, E. (1988). Character building: Transmitting values in schools. *Curriculum Review, 26*(1), 18–22.

CASE 2

Management Is Management: Or Is It?

The Shoreline School District is located on the banks of one of the Great Lakes in an industrial section of an upper-midwest state. It is a large school system containing 19,400 pupils, which has faced the enrollment declines common in many communities along the "rust belt." Despite a 10 percent reduction in enrollment over the past decade, the school district has maintained a positive attitude regarding quality programming; and steadfastly, the taxpayers have supported referenda to raise additional taxes for the schools.

Tim Anderson came to Shoreline just eleven months ago. A former middle school science teacher and middle school principal, he accepted the position of personnel director in Shoreline immediately following the completion of his doctorate in school administration. His youth, thirty-three years of age, and his enthusiasm were welcome additions to a much older administrative staff. Superintendent Alex Pryor saw to it that Tim had ample exposure in the community. He arranged for him to join the Rotary Club and scheduled him to give talks before a variety of civic groups. Dr. Pryor wanted the community to perceive Tim's youth and enthusiasm as indicators that, despite a downward trend in the local economy, the school district was still looking forward.

Tim's wife, Margie, and their two children readily adapted to Shoreline, a modest-sized city composed primarily of established neighborhoods. Although still a very industrial-based community, it is one of those rare cities able to attract middle- and upper-middle-class residents. This is due largely to the beaches and other water recreation opportunities. The Andersons purchased a home just two blocks from the water front and became friends with most of their new neighbors.

Perhaps Tim's closed friend in Shoreline is Bill Stanton, a business executive who lives next door. Bill and Tim are about the same age. They share many of the same interests. Bill is also a personnel director, but for Shoreline Metal Products. Although they occupy positions having a common title, their academic preparation for the two jobs is substantially different. Bill graduated from a small liberal arts college in Pennsylvania with a major in business. He them completed a law degree in Washington, DC. After working at a large law firm in the nation's capital for six years, Bill decided to seek different experiences. The position with Shoreline, a company racked by labor problems over the past twelve years, provided an attractive salary and a host of difficult problems. Tim, on the other hand, earned three degrees at the same large state university. In fact, Tim had never resided outside of his home state.

One sunny October day while the two were out on the lake sailing, Tim mentioned that it seemed likely the school district would have to reduce its force by twenty-five teachers before the next school year. Dwindling resources and students combined to squeeze the fiscal resources of the district.

"That shouldn't be all that difficult," Bill commented. "You have a master contract. Doesn't it contain a provision for making reduction in force decisions?"

"That's true," answered Tim. "However, our contract calls for us to form a joint committee between the teachers union and the administration to determine if reductions are necessary and how they will be carried out."

Bill looked astonished. "You have to be pulling my leg. Who in their right mind would ever agree to something like that. Establishing a committee and letting them decide which reductions are necessary takes away management's ability to make personnel decisions."

"I know," Tim replied. "But that language has been in our contract for a long time."

Bill's comments weighed heavily on Tim. Several days after their discussion he went in to see Dr. Pryor and brought up the matter of the reduction in force provision in the master contract.

"Dr. Pryor, I've been thinking about our last administrative meeting where we discussed the likelihood that we are going to have to reduce twenty-five positions in our district before next school year. I'm bothered by the language in our master contract regarding how reduction in force decisions are to be made. Could you tell me how this provision of a joint committee got into the contract?" Tim asked.

Dr. Pryor walked over and picked up his copy of the contract and slowly turned to the page containing the language about reductions. He read it silently and when he finished he looked up at Tim. "What's the problem? This is the same language that we have had for the past seven years. What is it about the language that bothers you?"

"I'm not really sure," Tim responded. "Maybe its the ambiguity of the statement. What occurs if we can't agree with the teachers union? How is the matter decided?"

Superintendent Pryor's glasses were on the tip of his nose and, looking above the rim, his eyes focused on Tim as he spoke. "That's never happened here. We had to reduce teachers four of the last seven years and it's never happened. We always find a way to compromise—to work it out. If we have good data indicating our need to reduce staff, the teachers have worked with us."

Tim left the superintendent's office feeling more assured. Maybe his friend, Bill, just didn't understand teachers. After all, many were lifelong residents in Shoreline and took a great deal of pride in the school system. That evening Tim saw Bill barbecuing in the back yard and walked over to talk to him.

"Bill, the other day you commented about the school system's reduction in force policy. You were pretty critical. Your comments led me to give this matter a great deal of thought. Could you be more specific about why you think our policy will not work?" Tim requested.

"Sure. For one thing, you can't do anything unless the other side agrees. That's bad management. What if they decide that you do not need to let any teachers go. Are you going to go along with that? Are the union bosses willing to share the blame if you go bankrupt because you didn't let teachers go? It's as simple as that."

"Here in Shoreline, the administrators have been able to compromise with the union in the past. Alex Pryor assured me that they are objective and will look at facts and figures. If we can prove our need to reduce staff, they have cooperated. So the policy has worked." Tim explained.

"Look, Tim, unions look out for their members. You are supposed to look out for the organization. These are two different goals. Compromise will eventually result in serious problems. You cannot have fifty different people deciding the course of action for the school system. Somebody's got to be in charge—to make difficult decisions. Compromise, my friend, is a dangerous practice. It's an easy way out of making a difficult decision."

Tim still wasn't convinced. He asked further, "Don't you think workers ought to have some say so in what happens to them? Since they are the ones who stand to lose their jobs, shouldn't they be allowed to play a role in these decisions?"

"And what do you expect, Tim? You think they are going to say its fine for you to take away their jobs. Of course not. I think you have been set up. This contract is unmanageable. If you have to reduce your teaching force with that language, I suggest you convince your superintendent to get directly involved. Let him be the one who reaches the compromises. Then he can't blame the negative results on you."

Obviously, Tim respected Bill's opinion. He wouldn't be wasting his time asking all these questions if he didn't see him as somewhat of an expert in labor relations. On the other hand, Tim also admired his boss, Dr. Pryor. He perceived the superintendent to be a man of wisdom who utilized his thirty years of experience to the fullest. In just one week, Tim would be forced to notify the union president of the intent to reduce the teaching force and to commence the operations of the joint committee as specified in the master contract. His self-confidence in his ability to handle his job had been greatly reduced by his neighbor's assessment of the task before him.

Tim agonized about the proper course of action. With no time left for weighing alternatives, he called Jane Sparkman, president of the teachers' union, and notified her of the need to form the committee. She reacted with surprise.

"I thought we were over these reductions. When is this going to stop? The last time we were cooperative. This time, we may have to say, no. Here we are just two months into a new school year and you are already talking about the need to let more teachers go." Immediately following these comments, Mrs. Sparkman said good-bye.

Tim called Bill at his office and told him what had occurred. Bill responded confidently, "Isn't that what I predicted? Forget about what's happened in the past. Unions are very unpredictable entities. They respond on the basis of economic and political considerations. They're not terribly committed to philosophical principles."

"What do you think I should do?" Tim asked.

Bill answered, "You have to convince your boss that this provision will not work. You are probably going to end up in court over this one. I'd play tough. Tell the union that you have no room for compromise. Tell them you have to reduce twenty-five teachers and you welcome their input as to how it should be done. But I would be firm that they are only giving advice, not making the decisions. Also, I'd be sure that they understand that the need to reduce twenty-five employees is not a negotiable item; you only want their input with regards to how it should be accomplished."

Tim hung up the phone and went immediately to see the superintendent. He informed his superior of his intention to be tough with the teachers. He relayed Mrs. Sparkman's negative reaction to his suggestion to form the committee and reasserted his belief that the contract language would not work. The disappointment on Dr. Pryor's face was obvious.

"Tim, maybe I expected too much from you. You have to understand that unions always say they can't agree to things. But somehow we always manage to work it out. This school district isn't U.S. Steel. Teachers are taxpayers. They have friends on the school board. They affect elections. We have learned to work together here in Shoreline. You need to learn that or think about finding another job." With that sobering comment, the superintendent ended the brief discussion.

THE CHALLENGE: Place yourself in Tim's position. What would you do at this point?

KEY ISSUES/QUESTIONS:

1. Why do you think Dr. Pryor and Bill have such different opinions about the effectiveness of the school district's policy regarding reduction in force?
2. To what extent are principles and practices of management in private industry applicable to public service organizations?
3. Identify factors that differentiate the Shoreline School District from the Shoreline Metal Company.

4. Should Tim be discussing school business with Bill?

5. Is Bill correct when he makes the judgment that the school administrators cannot rely on past successes in working with the union? Why or why not?

6. Assess Dr. Pryor's behavior in this case. Do you think his behavior is appropriate?

7. Identify environmental factors that should be weighed in making the decision.

8. Identify alternatives that are available to Tim given the circumstances, and evaluate the potential effectiveness of each.

9. Is Bill correct when he states that unions look out for their members and managers are supposed to look out for the organization?

SUGGESTED READINGS:

Allen, R., & Nixon, B. (1988). Developing a new approach to leadership. *Management Education and Development, 19*(3), 174–186.

Burke, R. (1983). Don't be a slave to seniority when developing RIF procedures. *American School Board Journal, 170*(7), 20–21.

Castetter, W. (1986). *The personnel function in educational administration* (4th ed.), pp. 180–183. New York: Macmillan.

Collins, P., & Nelson, D. (1983). Reducing the teacher workforce: A management perspective. *Journal of Law and Education, 12*(2), 249–272.

Conway, J. (1984). The myth, mystery and mastery of participative decision making in education. *Educational Administrative Quarterly, 20*(3), 11–40.

Dunnerstick, R. (1987). If RIFs are in the cards for your schools, deal with them deftly. *American School Board Journal, 174*(1), 34.

Eberts, R. (1987). Union-negotiated employment rules and teacher quits. *Economics of Education Review, 6*(1), 15–25.

Hanson, E. (1985). *Educational administration and organizational behavior* (2nd ed.), pp. 157–162. Boston: Allyn & Bacon.

Hartley, M. (1985). Leadership style and conflict resolution: No manager is an island. *Journal of Cooperative Education, 21*(2), 16–23.

Kowalski, T. (1982). Don't be duped by the industrial mystique. *Executive Educator, 4*(11), 46.

Lieberman, M. (1986). *Beyond public education,* chap. 2. New York: Praeger.

Parkay, F. (1984). A conceptual model for quality oriented educational leadership. *Planning and Changing, 15*(1), 3–9.

Snyder, K., & Anderson, R. (1987). What principals can learn from corporate management. *Principal, 66*(4), 22–26.

Threadgill, R. (1988). Analyzing the financial impact of teacher attrition and retirement. *Planning and Changing, 19*(3), 8–13.

Wengert, M. (1985). *Dismissal of tenured faculty due to financial exigency.* Unpublished Ed.D. thesis, Pepperdine University, California.

Williams, M. (1985). The management of conflict. *New Directions for Higher Education, 13*(2), 33–36.

Wood, C. (1982). Financial exigencies and the dismissal of public school teachers: A legal perspective. *Government Union Review, 3*(4), 49–66.

CASE 3

Setting Higher Standards

THE COMMUNITY

Simpson is a community with approximately 18,000 residents located in a southern state. It has a hospital, a community college, one manufacturing plant, and the usual collection of small retail businesses. Located in a predominately farming area (dairy products and cotton), it has experienced little growth in the past decade. Most citizens are content with the community's status, and there have not been any major initiatives to attract industry or residents. Taxes are relatively low, and most citizens want their community to remain essentially the same.

THE SCHOOL DISTRICT

The Simpson Public School District consists of seven elementary schools, a junior high school, and a high school. Enrolling a total of 3,476 students in grades kindergarten through twelve, the district has had a stable enrollment for the last five years. In many ways, Simpson is an average district. Student achievement scores, property taxes, and even the number of high school graduates going on to college are at or near the average for the state. The district is governed by a seven-member school board. Members are elected to four-year terms in a nonpartisan election held in May. The terms of individuals are staggered to prevent a majority of the board being elected in any one year. The district superintendent, Jack Darble, is a twenty-seven-year employee. He has been in his current position for the past twelve years. Education has never really been a topic of controversy in

Simpson. Most citizens appear pleased with the schools. Many are enthusiastic boosters of Simpson High School athletics, especially the school's highly successful football team.

THE SCHOOL BOARD ELECTION

Two members of the school board were facing election. One of the two announced that he would not seek another term. The other one, Rose Connors, officially filed the papers for her candidacy on the first day that it was possible to do so. Two other candidates also filed for the election. All board seats in Simpson are filled on an at-large basis. That is, board members are not elected to represent designated areas of the school district. Accordingly, two of the three candidates would be seated on the board following the election. New terms of office commence July 1, the start of the fiscal year. In addition to Rose Conner and the board member not seeking reelection, the five other board members are:

- Peter Swaim, physician and current board president
- Jane Mason, housewife and current board vice-president
- Jimmy Lawton, farmer
- Arnold Barker, farmer
- Drew Wilson, insurance agent

The three candidates seeking the two seats were:

- Rose Connors, a biology instructor at the community college completing her first term as a board member
- George Jenkins, owner of Jenkins Farm Supply
- Elizabeth Potter, housewife and sister-in-law of George Jenkins

For the most part, there was little campaigning. There were no debates or public forums. Rose Connors distributed pamphlets in the community emphasizing her experience as a teacher and board member. Jenkins and Potter had some posters printed and paid for several ads in the local newspaper. Compared to school board elections in many other communities, this one was rather subdued. However, low-key school board elections were not unusual in Simpson. Often citizens would comment that they did not know why anyone wanted to be on the school board.

Jenkins and Potter spread the word among close friends that they deserved to be on the board because they were lifelong residents of Simpson. Mrs. Connors, on the other hand, moved to the town about six years ago when she and her husband accepted teaching positions at the community college. Mr. Jenkins, in particular, was well known in Simpson and had "connections" in statewide politics. When the votes were tallied, Jenkins and Potter won the two seats by a rather large margin. Less than 40 percent of the eligible voters came to the polls to vote in the school board election.

POSTELECTION ACTIVITIES

The school board election was held in early May and the two new members would not be seated until the first board meeting in July. Nevertheless, within three weeks of being elected, George Jenkins visited the five returning board members. It was common knowledge in the community that George was a close friend of the state's governor. One reward of that friendship was an appointment two years ago on the governor's select task force on educational reform. Surprisingly, George Jenkins barely mentioned this fact in his campaign for the school board. The experience on the governor's task force was bittersweet for him. Although he relished the public exposure, he was tremendously disappointed when the task force's recommendations were soundly rejected by the state legislature. When this occurred, George wrote letters to the editors of all the major newspapers in the state claiming that the rejection was simply a manifestation of partisan politics (the majority in the legislature is Democratic and the governor is a Republican). He tried to persuade the public that the recommendations of the task force were never fairly judged on the basis of their own merit.

During the visits with the board members, George rekindled his judgments regarding the role of partisan politics in the demise of the recommendations of the governor's task force. He also expressed his concern regarding the political clout of the state teachers' association, or "union" as he called it. He blamed this organization for the defeat of the governor's reform initiatives. He gave each of the board members a packet containing digests from several national reform reports. He urged them to study the material and join him in an effort to improve the Simpson Public Schools by adopting policies congruent with the recommendations of the former state task force.

Each of five returning board members agreed to meet with George, and each gave him the courtesy of listening to his views. Dr. Swaim was the only board member to caution George.

"You were just elected, and you'll have several years to introduce your ideas to other board members and the administration. Right now, I think you would be wise to take the time to study what has occurred in the school district and to identify areas where improvement is needed."

George Jenkins was not one who took advice well. He ignored the physician and continued with his visits. One of those visits was with the school superintendent. Although the two knew each other, their previous contact had been limited to official functions. When George Jenkins was serving on the governor's task force several years ago, he did call the superintendent once to get his opinions on several matters.

In confronting Superintendent Darble, George was more direct than he had been with the five board members. After again expressing his contempt for the political activities of educators, he astonished the superintendent with a five-point recommendation for school reform in Simpson:

1. All teachers were to receive two formal evaluations each school year. All those receiving less than satisfactory assessments would be identified at a public board meeting and forced to enter a remedial program.
2. All students scoring one grade level below current grade placement in either reading or mathematics competency would be retained in their present grade.
3. The school year would be extended five days this next school year and an additional five days the following school year.
4. Any student receiving a grade lower than a "C" in reading, mathematics, or science would be required to do remedial work in the summer.
5. All teachers would be required to assign daily homework.

Mr. Darble responded carefully, "Mr. Jenkins, several of these ideas have some merit. But, we can't just charge out and change things like this overnight. We have policies, contracts, and the like. Besides, each of these ideas should be studied independently. I am sure there are some dimensions of these recommendations that you have not considered."

"Well Darble," responded the newly elected official, "that's what's wrong with schools. If I sat around on my thumbs waiting for my employees and customers to tell me something was okay before I could do it, I would have been bankrupt years ago. By God, we're going to make Simpson a model for the rest of the state. The governor will point to this community with pride and tell the public about the school district that works. We can show the state what could have been accomplished if the governor's recommendations had been followed two years ago."

"I just don't think your ideas can be implemented, especially not in the next few months," answered the superintendent.

"We will see, Mr. Darble. We will see." And with those words, George Jenkins turned and left the superintendent's office.

During the next month, George concentrated on three of the returning board members. Following his initial visits, he decided that Dr. Swaim, Mr. Darble, and the board's vice-president, Mrs. Mason, were not going to be cooperative. Thus, he intensified his efforts with Lawson, Barker, and Wilson.

THE INCIDENT

Under the law in this state, each school board holds a reorganization meeting in early July. New board members are given the oath of office and officers are elected for the fiscal year. The school attorney administered the oath to the two new members, and then conducted the election of a new president. Mrs. Potter immediately nominated her brother-in-law, George Jenkins. Dr. Swaim in turn nominated Mrs. Mason. To the surprise of those present, Jenkins was elected by a margin of five to two. The fact that Mr. Wilson cast his vote for George Jenkins was the biggest surprise. Wilson had traditionally supported positions taken by the physician.

After being on the board for only about five minutes, George was now the elected leader of the seven-member group. Dr. Swaim handed his successor the gavel and the agenda prepared by the superintendent for the remainder of the meeting. Mr. Jenkins's first order of business was to conduct an election for vice-president. The other new board member, Mrs. Potter, was also elected by a five to two margin. Dr. Swaim and Mrs. Mason graciously congratulated the new officers and publicly announced they would work to promote progress and harmony on the school board.

Laying the agenda aside without even looking at it, George Jenkins announced that Mrs. Potter wanted to introduce a special item of business. She read from a prepared statement:

Ladies and gentlemen,

After considering many aspects of our community and school system, I think we need to move forward in improving our schools. In my mind this will be impossible unless we have leadership committed to change. That means a superintendent who is willing to take risks and is not intimidated by unions and other obstructionists. Mr. Darble has served this community for many years, and I do appreciate his efforts. The time has come, however, for new leadership. Therefore, I move that Mr. Darble be reassigned to a teaching post at the high school for the remaining two years of his contract. This board should honor the salary in that contract and he can be assigned to some duties in the summer to assure that he is earning his salary.

There was an immediate second from board member Lawton. A hush fell over the meeting. Dr. Swaim asked to be recognized.

"This is outrageous. First of all, this item is not even on the agenda. Second, there are no concrete reasons why Mr. Darble should be replaced. I object to these proceedings and ask our attorney to declare this matter out of order."

Before the attorney could speak, Mr. Jenkins slammed down his newly acquired gavel and said loudly, "I'm the one who decides what's in order at this meeting. Quite frankly, doctor, you had two years as president and little was done to institute reform in this district. The time has come for bold action. We need to improve our schools, and unfortunate as it is, this is where we start."

Mrs. Mason requested to hear specific reasons why Mr. Darble should be reassigned. Neither Mrs. Potter nor those supporting her motion were willing to do so. The vote was four to two in favor of reassigning the superintendent—Mr. Wilson abstained.

Disbelief turned to anger and Dr. Swaim stood and pointed his finger at George Jenkins, "You are going to destroy this school system and I will not be a party to it. I resign my seat on this board and I hope that the teachers and taxpayers of this community will react strongly and swiftly to the injustice that has occurred here this evening." With that said, he left the meeting.

George Jenkins responded as Dr. Swaim walked from the room while being applauded by the teachers present at the meeting, "That's your choice, doctor. Believe me, this action does not make me feel good. But my experiences dealing with education over the past two years have convinced me that change will only come if we take risks. School improvement is our goal and Mr. Darble has already indicated to me that he really doesn't want to be part of it."

Dejected, the superintendent announced he would follow the board's wishes and accept the assignment at the high school. One of his assistants was named acting superintendent until a replacement could be employed.

THE CHALLENGE: Assess the decision made by the superintendent. Do you agree with it? What would you have done if you were in his place?

KEY ISSUES/QUESTIONS:

1. To what extent were environmental factors (i.e., factors external to the school district as an organization) responsible for what occurred in this case?
2. Are public organizations more or less susceptible to environmental influences than private organizations?
3. Assess the superintendent's behavior following his first encounter with George Jenkins shortly after the board election. What would you have done differently?
4. There are at least two major legal issues included in this case:
   a. a school board's ability to reassign a superintendent even though he has two years remaining on his contract, and
   b. a school board's ability to take such action even though the item is not on the agenda. Are laws regarding these two matters the same in most states? What are the laws in your home state?
5. What positive outcomes might result from this incident?
6. To what extent is the community at-large responsible for what occurred in this case?
7. Identify all of the superintendent's available options regarding his reassignment.
8. Assess Dr. Swaim's behavior. Should he have done something after receiving his first visit from George Jenkins? Should he have resigned from the board?
9. Identify potential motivators with regard to George Jenkins's behavior. Why did he run for the board? What exactly is he trying to accomplish?
10. What are some possible explanations why three of the five returning board members voted with Jenkins and Potter?

SUGGESTED READINGS:

Bacal, E. (1986). Learn not to burn, or fulminate over school board trouble. *American School Board Journal, 173*(5), 29–30.

Bacharach, S., et al. (1986). The work environment and school reform. *Teachers College Record, 88,* 241–256.

Carr, R. (1988). Second-wave reforms crest at local initiative. *The School Administrator, 45*(7), 16–18.

Edwards, M. (1988). Setting school board goals: A model for accountability. *Educational Horizons, 66*(3), 117–118.

Henson, K. (1986). Reforming America's public schools. *USA Today, 114*(3), 75–77.

Hopkins, R. (1989). How to survive and succeed as the chief school executive. *The School Administrator, 9*(46), 15–17.

Hoy, W., & Ferguson, J. (1985). A theoretical framework and exploration of organizational effectiveness of schools. *Educational Administration Quarterly, 21*(2), 117–134.

Krajewski, R. (1983). Nine ways a superintendent can corral a maverick board member. *American School Board Journal, 170*(11), 29–30.

MacDougall, C. (1988). Boards need education, too! *Updating School Board Policies, 19*(5), 1–2.

Namit, C. (1987). How a crisis meeting can control school board trouble. *American School Board Journal, 174*(9), 36–37.

Niblett, S. (1985). *Superintendent turnover and organizational change.* Unpublished Ph.D. thesis, University of California, Santa Barbara.

Peterson, P. (1985). Did the education commissions say anything? *Education and Urban Society, 17*(2), 126–144.

Rada, R. (1984). Community dissatisfaction and school governance. *Planning and Changing, 15*(4), 234–247.

Roeder, G. (1987). *A study of the reasons why Michigan school superintendents were dismissed or encouraged to leave their positions between 1980 and 1985.* Unpublished Ph.D. thesis, University of Michigan, Ann Arbor.

Seashore, K., et al. (1988). Knowledge use and school improvement. *Curriculum Inquiry, 18*(1), 33–62.

Shanker, A. (1985). The reform reports: Reaction from the front lines. *Education and Urban Society, 17*(2), 215–222.

Slaughter, S. (1988). Academic freedom and the state: Reflections on the uses of knowledge. *Journal of Higher Education, 59*(3), 241–262.

Turlington, R. (1985). How testing is changing education in Florida. *Educational Measurement: Issues and Practices, 4*(2), 9–11.

Wimpelberg, R., & Ginsberg, R. (1985). Are school districts responding to *A Nation at Risk? Education and Urban Society, 17*(2), 196–203.

Yeakey, C., & Johnston, G. (1985). High school reform: A critique and a broader construct of social reality. *Education and Urban Society, 17*(2), 157–170.

CASE 4

Too Many Schools

THE COMMUNITY AND SCHOOL DISTRICT

The Albright County School District surrounds a city of 285,000 in the southern part of the United States. The city is located in the center of the county and has its own school system. Many local residents refer to the Albright County schools as the "doughnut" and to the city school system as the "hole in the doughnut." Although the city school system is substantially smaller than the county schools with regard to square miles, it has nearly four times as many students as the county system.

The Albright County School District was legally formed in 1959 when nine separate township school districts were consolidated. Since that time, a great many demographic changes have occurred in the county. In the 1960s and 1970s, many residents moved out of the city into new housing developments concentrated just outside the city limits (i.e., just outside the city boundaries and within the county school system). In part, the migration to the county could be attributed to a national movement toward suburban living. To a larger extent, the migration patterns in Albright County are products of two other considerations: (1) increasing taxes in the city, and (2) a growing dissatisfaction with the city school system.

Homebuyers find an attractive set of financial and social conditions existing in the county school system. The following are the most influential:

1. The county schools have substantially smaller enrollments than the city schools. There are no county high schools with enrollments over 1,500 students; yet, the city high schools are all beyond this enrollment mark.

2. Another factor is busing. The county schools transport virtually all students to and from school (including kindergarten). For many families, this is an attractive feature.

3. In the late 1960s and early 1970s, drug and alcohol abuse became concerns for many parents. The county schools, largely because of the rural character, are perceived to be "safer" environments. Parents view the county schools as having more rigid discipline and a more homogeneous population with regard to family income.

4. Taxes in the county are less than 50 percent of what they are in the city. In large measure, this difference is attributable to tax rates for services other than schools (e.g., libraries, fire protection, city government).

5. Most home builders (developers) find it profitable to concentrate on subdivisions in the county where land is less expensive and more easily approved for housing units.

Albright County is not a typical rural school district. The wealth of the school district, as measured by taxable property, is quite high. The largest industrial plant in the county was located outside the city; and even though this operation closed several years ago, there remains a number of smaller industries within the school district's boundaries. The amount of taxable property behind each student is substantially higher in the county than it is in the city.

Additionally, the topography of the county provides some attractive sites for developing middle- and upper-income housing. Three rivers meander through the county school system providing beautiful home sites.

In 1959, the Albright County schools had just 6,700 students. The data below exhibit what happened over the next two decades:

1959	6,700 pupils
1965	7,400 pupils
1970	8,500 pupils
1975	10,200 pupils
1980	14,050 pupils

Not surprisingly, the county schools were forced to engage in a rigorous building program. From 1959 to 1985 every school in the district was either completely renovated or replaced. Several new schools were erected. Facility development in the school district was largely controlled by political considerations related to keeping schools dispersed throughout the county. This remains an important consideration. The vast majority of the population growth occurred in a single township bordering the city limits. In most other townships, population, especially student population, remained stable or declined slightly. Yet, over the years, the school board refused to concentrate new buildings in the exact areas where the most growth was occurring. The preferred solution included two critical dimensions: (1) keep schools in the small towns (and townships) where they were already located, and (2) bus students from the one growth township to other parts of the county. Thus, as schools in small towns needed renovation or replacement, no consideration was given to population shifts in the school district.

Building new schools or improving existing facilities has never been much of a problem for the Albright County schools. State laws governing school construction place all the burden for financing construction on local taxpayers. The school district has a very high assessed valuation, so it is able to generate revenues for school construction without extremely large tax increases.

In fall 1980, the county school system consisted of the following attendance centers:

- 3 high schools, grades 9–12
- 2 junior/senior high schools, grades 7–12
- 3 middle schools, grades 7–8
- 15 elementary schools, grades K–6

Given that the enrollment was at an all time high in 1980, the school officials continued to pursue capital development, believing that the demographic patterns of the past two decades would continue. In the early 1980s, one of the junior/senior high schools with an enrollment of only 650 students was completely renovated at a cost of $15 million.

In fall 1981, the school administrators were shocked when the district's enrollment dropped for the first time. There were 460 fewer pupils than the previous September (1980). The decline included a rather significant decline in kindergarten enrollments. After examining the problem, the superintendent and board decided that the drop was a temporary phenomenon resulting because some parents opted for parochial education (there were two Catholic and two Lutheran elementary schools within the boundaries of the county district and students also had access to two Catholic high schools and one Lutheran high school in the city).

In early December 1981, the school officials received another unpleasant surprise. The large truck manufacturing plant in the school district announced it was closing its operations and moving to another state. Not only did this plant employ over 2,000 workers, its assets constituted about 25 percent of the school district's assessed valuation.

THE PROBLEM

The 1981–82 school year was a period the officials of the Albright County School District would like to forget. Superintendent Harry Carson had reached retirement age and departed in spring 1982. A national search for a successor was executed and on July 1, 1982, Dr. Jerome Bellman assumed the role of chief executive of the school district. Dr. Bellman was originally from New England but moved to this southern state to complete his doctoral work. Over the past eleven years, he has remained in the state in three different school districts, in one as a principal, in another as assistant superintendent, and in the third as superintendent.

Dr. Bellman brought experience and objectivity to the superintendency in Albright County. After familiarizing himself with the school system in the first three months on the job, he recommended that the school board approve a planning study to be conducted by a planning team consisting of three university professors. He convinced the board that an objective analysis of facilities, enrollments, finances, and educational programs was necessary if strategic planning was to occur.

From November 1982 to June 1983, the three professors examined the school district. They issued their report to the superintendent and board at a regular school board meeting during summer 1983. The following were among the more cogent findings:

1. The school district enrollment was likely to remain in a declining pattern for at least the next decade. A declining birth rate, the withdrawal of industry, and unfavorable interest rates on mortgage loans were cited as prominent causes.
2. The minority population in the school district had increased from 1.5 percent in 1975 to 6 percent in 1983. Virtually all of this increase was due to the relocation of black families from the city to a housing subdivision just outside the city limits.
3. The utilization levels of some of the schools had dropped below 70 percent. This was especially true in the less populated areas of the county, that is, in the small town schools.
4. There was a growing discrepancy in curricular offerings in the high schools.
5. The school district was likely to face financial problems for the first time in its existence. The closing of the truck plant alone was estimated to result in a drop of $80 million in assessed valuation.

These and other findings led the consultants to recommend that the school district close at least one high school and one elementary school in the next three years. Additionally, it was recommended that school closings ought to be done in a fashion that considered all needs of the school district (a systems approach). In particular, the consultants urged the school officials to address the issues related to a growing minority population and inequalities in high school curricula.

Following the report, Dr. Bellman was able to get the board to agree to close an elementary school. This school, however, was not one of the remotely located schools, but an older school located in the township having the most growth. The board persisted in its refusal to close any elementary schools identified with outlying communities or to close any of the high schools. The board president told the local newspaper that it was just too early to conclude that the population would continue to decline and that closing the one elementary school was a sufficient response to the planning study recommendations.

Enrollments during the following two school years continued to drop. Financial problems were indeed on the horizon for the school district. Dr. Bellman and his central office staff placed a high priority on raising teacher salaries to a level comparable to the city school system and they realized that the underutilization of schools constituted one barrier to that goal.

In October 1985, Dr. Bellman recommended that the board approve funding for an even more extensive planning study than the one conducted two years previously. He did so because two key population trends identified in the first study not only proved to be correct, but were more significant than the consultants had projected. The two trends were the decline in overall enrollment and the increase in minority enrollment. The board consented and another consultant team consisting of the three original university professors plus three additional consultants (two additional professors and a black school superintendent from another state) was retained. The scope of examination was expanded and a special focus was given to studying the implications of a growing minority enrollment within a school district with an overall decline in students.

After one year of analyzing data, the consultant team issued a 500-page report reaffirming earlier findings. This time, however, the professors recommended closing two of the five high schools. Overall utilization of the facilities had dropped to 60 percent, and one high school was now below a 50 percent utilization level (i.e., there were 920 students in a school designed for 2,000). The growth in minority population surged in the concentrated area identified in the 1983 study. The elementary school serving this area was now 54 percent black and the junior high school was 61 percent black. The district had an overall minority enrollment of only 10 percent. Some schools remained void of any minority students. Finances and curricula continued to be two major concerns.

The second strategic planning report was greeted with skepticism by some school board members. The doubters continued to cling to the notion that population growth was just around the corner. Privately, the school board told Dr. Bellman and his staff that (before making any decisions on the recommendations to close additional schools) they wanted to wait to see what would occur over the next two years.

In each of the following two school years, 1986–87 and 1987–88, the administration of the school district updated the data bases generated by the consultants in their two studies. These updates suggested that, if anything, the professors were consistently conservative in estimating enrollment declines. Three significant trends persisted: (1) overall enrollments continued to drop about 3 to 4 percent per year; (2) minority enrollments continued to increase by about 5 percent per year and the students were concentrated in one subdivision; (3) one township continued to grow while the other six declined but the board bused students to the schools rather than relocating the attendance centers.

Dr. Bellman became concerned about desegregation because two schools now had a minority-majority even though the overall minority enrollment in the district remained only about 13 percent. A plan was put in place to bus some minority children to outlying schools, but school closings remained unacceptable to a majority of the school board.

In fall 1988, Dr. Bellman again met with officials of the teachers' union and his administrative staff to outline the problems. Those present were unified in the belief that something had to be done. In October 1988, Dr. Bellman once again outlined the figures for the school board and, once again, they indicated that they were not prepared to close a single high school, let alone two. The board did agree to a series of public hearings that would allow Dr. Bellman and his staff to describe the problems to the public. Dr. Bellman had the support of about 90 percent of this staff because he had publicly linked the issue of closing schools with concerns for curricular equity and higher employee salaries.

For the most part, residents of the outlying areas who believed their schools might be closed attended these hearings. They questioned the accuracy of demographic projections and retained their own consultants, several university professors who largely ignored the management issues facing the school district but testified that small schools were wonderful environments for children. The reactions of the public in these hearings had a profound effect on the school board members. Their belief that closing a high school would be political suicide was reinforced. For a third time, they informally let Dr. Bellman know that they would not support closing a high school and urged him to pursue alternatives to deal with the financial, educational, and racial balance problems identified through strategic planning.

The school board members' refusal to act on the recommendations to close one or two high schools was not indicative of the respect the board members held for Dr. Bellman. Except for the issue of school closings, the board supported the superintendent by approving his recommendations. In fact, the board openly praised the superintendent for his leadership on numerous occasions. In 1986, for example, the board found out Dr. Bellman was a finalist for another superintendency and they immediately approved a 10 percent increase in his salary and awarded him a five-year contract. He decided to stay in Albright County.

Despite these obvious indications of support, the board steadfastly refused to heed the superintendent's advice with regard to school closings. Dr. Bellman became increasingly dejected over this fact. He knew that the district would one day reach a point where it could no longer fund all of this unused space. More importantly, he realized that as long as this problem remained unresolved he could not improve teacher salaries and pursue educational innovations he believed to be necessary. So despite all the praises and personal raises, he feared that one day it would all come tumbling down.

THE CHALLENGE: Place yourself in Dr. Bellman's position. What would you do?

KEY ISSUES/QUESTIONS:

1. Identify Dr. Bellman's options. What do you perceive to be the advantages and disadvantages of each?

2. Why do you believe the school board members are reluctant to close a high school?

3. Was it a good idea to have university professors complete the planning studies that led to the recommendations for school closings?

4. The parents who object to closing a high school retained two consultants to testify that small high schools are better than large high schools. Do you agree with this assessment? What evidence can you provide to support your answer?

5. Why do you believe that the teachers' union is supporting Dr. Bellman in this matter?

6. Why do taxpayers often fight to retain schools in small rural communities?

7. The state in which this occurred utilizes a program of total local funding for capital outlay. What are the range of options for financing facility projects that exist among the fifty states? Did the program of total local funding affect decisions in this case?

8. If you were Dr. Bellman, would you emphasize or deemphasize the fact that the teachers' union supported your position?

9. What is the relevance of the minority enrollment patterns present in the school district?

10. What is the relevance of curricular inequities among the five high schools in this case?

11. Should a community have the right to say no to school closings or should the state step-in and play a role in this matter?

SUGGESTED READINGS:

Boyd, W., & Wheaton, D. (1983). Conflict management in declining school districts. *Peabody Journal of Education, 50*(2), 25–36.

Bozza, R. (1985). *Declining enrollments and school closings: The management of political conflict.* Unpublished Ed.D. thesis, Rutgers, State University of New Jersey.

Chabotar, K. (1987). Use of financial forecasting in educational retrenchment. *Journal of Education Finance, 12,* 351–368.

Chabotar, K., & Dentler, R. (1985). Cutback management planning assistance for local public school systems. *Planning and Changing, 16,* 223–240.

Cibulka, J. (1987). Theories of education budgeting: Lessons from management of decline. *Educational Administration Quarterly, 23*(4), 7–40.

Crespo, M., & Hache, J. (1982). The management of decline in education: The case of Quebec. *Educational Administration Quarterly, 18*(1), 75–99.

Darling, J., & Ishler, R. (1989–90). Strategic conflict management: A problem-oriented approach. *National Forum of Educational Administration and Supervision Journal, 7*(1), 87–103.

Guthrie, J., & Reed, R. (1986). *Educational administration and policy,* pp. 52–55. Englewood Cliffs, NJ: Prentice-Hall.

Hayden, J. (1986). Crisis at the helm. *The School Administrator, 43*(10), 17–19.

Love, D. (1987). *Criteria and processes used in school-closing decisions by school corporations in Indiana.* Unpublished Ed.D. thesis, Indiana University, Bloomington.

Mertz, C. (1986). Conflict and frustration for school board members. *Urban Education, 20*(4), 397–418.

Newman, D., et al. (1987). Factors influencing the decision-making process: An examination of the effect of contextual variables. *Studies in Educational Evaluation, 13*(2), 199–209.

Nocera, E. (1986). *A study of school closing in two school systems in relation to decision-making and organizational and political impacts*. Unpublished Ph.D. thesis, University of Connecticut.

Owens, R., & Lewis, E. (1976). Managing participation in organizational decisions. *Group and Organizational Studies, 1,* 55–56.

Pankake, A., & Bailey, M. (1986). Managing decline in public schools. *Urban Education, 21,* 180–188.

Vroom, V., & Jago, A. (1988). *The new leadership: Managing participation in organizations,* pp. 54–65. Englewood Cliffs, NJ: Prentice-Hall.

Yukl, G. (1989). *Leadership in organizations* (2nd ed.), pp. 58–60. Englewood Cliffs, NJ: Prentice-Hall.

An Assistant Principal Who Does Not Fit the Image

THE COMMUNITY

Thomas Creek is an established suburb located approximately twelve miles from a major city in the western part of New York state. With its quiet tree-lined streets and attractive homes, Thomas Creek is definitely an upper-middle-class community. Most adult residents are college graduates; many hold prominent management positions; about 15 percent are self-employed professionals (e.g., lawyers, physicians, architects). Athough somewhat homogeneous with regard to family income, the community's population is diverse in other respects. Official census data provide the following population profile:

- Caucasian—73 percent
- Asian-American—13 percent
- Black—7 percent
- Hispanic—2 percent
- Other—1 percent

Unofficial data collected in a recent sociological study conducted by a local university indicate the following religious affiliations for the citizens of Thomas Creek:

- Protestant—34 percent
- Roman Catholic—26 percent
- Other Christian—3 percent
- Jewish—32 percent

- Moslem—3 percent
- Other or No Affiliation—2 percent

The overall population of the community is stable; there is very little land remaining for new developments.

THE SCHOOL SYSTEM

The brochure prepared by the Thomas Creek Chamber of Commerce identifies the public school system as a major asset of the community. The kindergarten through twelve system has maintained an outstanding reputation. The high school, for example, has won several citations from state and national groups for excellence in educational programming. The Chamber of Commerce publicity brochures include the following statement, "Thomas Creek—a community where cultural diversity and public education are strengths."

The public school system in Thomas Creek includes three elementary schools (K–5), a middle school (6–8), and a high school (9–12). The overall enrollment is 2,500 students. The number of students in the system has declined steadily since 1976 when the total enrollment was 3,150. In the past two years the enrollments have remained quite stable. In addition to the public schools, there are two private elementary schools located within the boundaries of the public school system: (1) St. Jerome Catholic School (K–6), and (2) Thomas Creek Academy (K–5).

THE HIGH SCHOOL

Although all the schools in Thomas Creek are considered well above the national average for public schools, it is the high school that remains the showpiece of the community's commitment to education. The facility is attractive, and although now twenty-seven years old, it has been constantly updated. Just recently fiber optics, two electronic classrooms, and two additional computer laboratories were added.

The curriculum at the school is somewhat comprehensive; technical and vocational courses are not as prevalent here as they are in the urban schools. The primary instructional thrust is college preparation. Approximately 80 percent of the high school graduates go on to four-year colleges and universities (another 10 percent go on to two-year institutions). The school offers a very comprehensive athletic program, having seven boys and seven girls athletic teams. With an enrollment of 870, the school also provides a myriad of clubs, fine arts, and related activities.

The staff is considered an asset. Most have advanced degrees, and there is very little turnover in the teaching positions. In the past five years, only three new teachers have been employed. But perhaps the most recognized symbol of excellence at the high school is Principal Allen Miller.

THE PRINCIPAL

Allen Miller accepted the principalship at Thomas Creek High School nine years ago. He held a similar position in a suburban high school outside of Cleveland, Ohio. He is an energetic person who frequently devotes twelve hours per day to his job. His extroverted personality, understanding demeanor, and patience have served him well in his current position. Parents, students, teachers, and other administrators generally perceive him to be a forceful leader. It is not surprising that he devotes much of the work day to meeting with students, teachers, and parents. His weekly coffee sessions with parents are highly publicized. By contrast, Allen spends very little time with what he calls "the administrivia" of running a high school—bus schedules, lunch programs, book rental, and the like. He not only does not like this type of work, he believes that he does not do very well with routine management tasks. The assignments Allen finds to be less exciting are assigned to Assistant Principal George Hopkins.

THE ASSISTANT PRINCIPAL

George Hopkins has worked at Thomas Creek High School for the last twenty-seven years. He was football coach and taught physical education prior to becoming an administrator. He has been assistant principal for the past fourteen years. He is considered the "enforcer" by the students—the person who hands out penalties. Mr. Hopkins's crewcut hairstyle and serious manner put his outward appearance in sharp contrast to Mr. Miller's corporate executive–type looks. Students often joke that Mr. Hopkins has two sets of clothing: wrinkled and more wrinkled. Despite these overt differences in the two administrators, they are respectful of each other and their personal relationship is congenial. Allen has recommended George for the highest level of merit increase for the last six years. In large measure this is due to Allen's recognition that his assistant is an essential complement of his own leadership style. George rarely disagrees with Allen and has accepted the role that has been created for him.

OTHER ADMINISTRATORS

Allen's immediate supervisor, Dr. Valerie Daniels, associate superintendent, and the superintendent, Dr. Ronald O'Brien, are very supportive of his leadership style at the high school. On several occasions, they have nominated him for outstanding administrator awards. In return, Allen respects Dr. Daniels who he believes is an effective leader. His contact with Dr. O'Brien has been somewhat limited; however, his perceptions of the superintendent are extremely positive. Dr. Daniels has been in Thomas Creek four years. She is a former elementary school principal in another district. Superintendent O'Brien has been at Thomas Creek just two years. He was a superintendent in a midwestern suburb prior to accepting his current position.

The principals meet once every two weeks with the associate superintendent. On rare occasions, the superintendent attends these sessions. Usually his presence at the meetings is related to a special issue, one he chooses to discuss directly with the principals. The formal relationship of the administrative staff is outlined in the following line-and-staff chart:

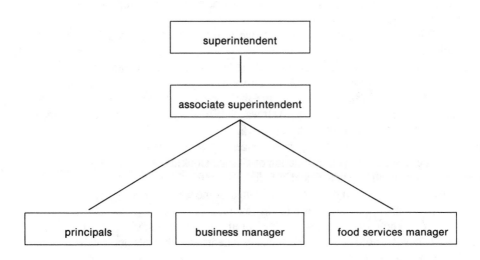

EVALUATION PROCEDURES

Performance evaluations for the school principals are conducted by the associate superintendent, who then discusses the outcomes with the individual principals in an evaluation conference. The superintendent attends each of these conferences. The superintendent makes decisions on salary increases based on input obtained from the associate superintendent. Typically the administrative staff receive higher percentage increases than other employees. On occasion the teachers' union attacks this practice, but their displeasure seems to have no effect on either the superintendent's recommendations or the board's approval of those recommendations. As part of the evaluation process, principals are required to evaluate their assistants and to bring the written documentation of that process to their own evaluation conferences. Each principal reviews subordinate evaluations with the associate superintendent and superintendent. The principal also makes a salary recommendation for assistant principals.

THE INCIDENT

Evaluation conferences for the principals are scheduled in late March of each year. When Allen Miller arrived at the central office for his appointment, he was not thinking about the evaluation. They had become so routine that his mind was concentrating on the agenda for the seniors' honor banquet that would take place in three weeks. He said hello to the secretaries as he arrived at the superintendent's office and went to the workroom to get a cup of coffee. Then he took a seat outside of Dr. O'Brien's office and his thoughts once again focused on the honors banquet. About five minutes later the door to the superintendent's office opened and Valerie Daniels emerged.

"Good morning, Allen. Come in, we're pretty much on schedule today," she said.

Allen smiled, nodded, and entered the large office. He exchanged pleasantries with the superintendent and took his customary seat (every evaluation conference found the three participants occupying the same seats around a small conference table as if the chairs were reserved). It was 9:35 A.M. and Allen figured that as usual he would be back in his office by 11:00 A.M.

Dr. Daniels was the first to speak once they were seated.

"Let's start with your evaluation of George Hopkins."

Mechanically, Allen ticked off the ratings for the various categories for his assistant. Most were in the "excellent" range; some were "above average"; and only one, personal appearance, was rated as "average."

"You know old coaches," Allen commented with a smile and a nod, "they always look like old coaches. Fortunately parents and students don't judge George by the way he looks."

The two central office administrators did not smile at Allen's comment; and being observant, Allen quickly retracted his grin. As the three sat silently, Allen began to get the feeling that something was wrong.

Dr. Daniels looked squarely at Allen and said, "This is a special community. Thomas Creek High School is a special secondary school. We have become increasingly concerned about the image our administrators present to the general public. In this regard, George has become somewhat of an embarrassment. He never wears a suit; he looks like he shaves before he goes to bed rather than in the morning; and he is not involved in any community service activities. Visitors to the school could easily mistake him for a custodian."

Allen thought this assessment was a bit harsh. He did not disagree with his supervisor's assessment, but he wondered why personal traits had suddenly become such a big issue. He asked,

"If you felt this strongly about George, why did you approve maximum merit raises for him the last few years?"

The superintendent decided to field the question, "I can only speak for last year. We did it for you, Allen. We did it for you. We didn't want you to feel hurt because we wouldn't accept your recommendation."

"So what does all this mean?" Allen inquired.

"It means," Dr. Daniels answered, "that George has got to go. We have an opening at the middle school for a physical education teacher. He can be assigned there. We'll see that he gets some driver education work in the summer to help with his overall salary."

"I just don't think this is right." Allen asserted. "George is a good administrator. I could not get along without him and I mean that. If anything, he has never received the recognition he deserves. I doubt that I can be as effective with someone else. I just feel terrible about this."

Dr. O'Brien again entered the conversation, "Allen, listen. You don't have to take the blame for this. We are willing to explain to the board that it is our decision. George won't be angry with you. He'll direct his outrage at me and perhaps Valerie—but not you. All we are asking from you is to be silent on the matter. It would not look good for you to be publicly fighting this decision."

"He's right, Allen," Dr. Daniels interjected. "You have a great thing going at Thomas Creek High School. But if you had an assistant whose image was congruent with that of the school district, you could be doing even more. Believe me, Dr. O'Brien and I have given this a great deal of thought. We want your assurance that you will go along. We are just asking you not to comment on the matter publicly. We'll take care of the rest."

THE CHALLENGE: Place yourself in Allen's position. What would you do in this situation?

KEY ISSUES/QUESTIONS:

1. To what extent do you believe the nature of the community plays a role in this case?
2. What aspects of organizational theory are helpful in determining why the personal appearance of an assistant principal is a critical element in this case?
3. What does Allen have to gain by agreeing to do what the superintendent and associate superintendent are requesting?
4. What options does Allen have, if any, beyond either agreeing or not agreeing to do what his superiors have asked of him?
5. Evaluate the administrative structure (line and staff) in this district. What do you like about it? What do you dislike?
6. To what extent is the line-and-staff relationship among the administrative staff a contributing factor to this case?
7. How do you assess the role of the associate superintendent in this case?
8. To what extent did Allen err by assuming that this would be a routine conference?
9. Some administrators might defend the action of the superintendent and assistant superintendent on the grounds that it is best to "act swiftly and forcefully" in controversial situations. Do you agree?
10. Discuss the differences between summative and formative evaluation. To what extent are the superintendent and associate superintendent supporting both processes?

SUGGESTED READINGS:

Aidala, G. (1986). *A study of career bound and place bound assistant principals in the public secondary schools of New York state and a comparison of their levels of job satisfaction.* Unpublished Ed.D. thesis, State University of New York, Albany.

Drake, T., & Roe, W. (1986). *The principalship* (3rd ed.). pp. 19–29. New York: Macmillan.

Fulton, O. (1987). Basic competencies of the assistant principal. *NASSP Bulletin, 71*(501), 52.

Hamner, T., & Turk, J. (1987). Organizational determinants of leader behavior and authority. *Journal of Applied Psychology, 72,* 647–682.

Hanson, E. (1985). *Educational administration and organizational behavior* (2nd ed.), pp. 168–169. Boston: Allyn and Bacon.

Harrison, W., & Peterson, K. (1988). Evaluation of principals: The process can be improved. *NASSP Bulletin, 72*(508), 1–4.

Hoy, W., & Forsyth, P. (1986). *Effective supervision: Theory into practice.* pp. 120–122. New York: Random House.

Hoy, W., & Miskel, C. (1987). *Educational administration: Theory, research and practice* (3rd ed.), pp. 76–79. New York: Random House.

Hoy, W., Newland, W., & Blaxovsky, R. (1977). Subordinate loyalty to superior, esprit, and aspects of bureaucratic structure. *Educational Administration Quarterly, 13*(1), 71–85.

Immegart, G. (1988). Leadership and leader behavior. In N. Boyan (Ed.), *Handbook of research on educational administration,* pp. 259–278. White Plains, NY: Longman.

Lang, R. (1986). The hidden dress code dilemma. *Clearing House, 59*(6), 277–279.

McCarthy, M. (1987). *The work-life of the assistant principal in public comprehensive high schools.* Unpublished Ed.D. thesis, University of Massachusetts.

McPherson, R., & Crowson, R. (1987). Sources of constraints and opportunities for discretion in the principalship. In J. Lane & H. Walberg (Eds.), *Effective school leadership,* pp. 129–156. Berkeley, CA: McCutchan.

Manatt, R. (1987). Lessons from a comprehensive performance appraisal project. *Educational Leadership, 44*(7), 8–14.

Newell, C. (1978). *Human behavior in educational administration,* chap. 6. Englewood Cliffs, NJ: Prentice-Hall.

Niehouse, O. (1988). Leadership concepts for the principal: A practical approach. *NASSP Bulletin, 72*(505), 50–52.

Norton, M., & Kriekard, (1987). Real and ideal competencies for the assistant principal. *NASSP Bulletin, 71*(501), 23–30.

Peterson, K. (1984). Mechanisms of administrative control over managers in educational organizations. *Administrative Science Quarterly, 29,* 573–597.

Wood, C., Nicholson, E., & Findley, D. (1985). *The secondary school principal: Manager and supervisor* (2nd ed.), chap. 4. Boston, Allyn & Bacon.

Yukl, G. (1989). *Leadership in organizations* (2nd ed.), pp. 151–157, 174–191. Englewood Cliffs, NJ: Prentice-Hall.

CASE 6

Program Expansion or Budget Cuts?

After serving four years as an assistant superintendent for instruction in a school district of 9,000 students, Lorraine Marcum decided it was time to pursue a superintendency. She carefully mulled over the myriad of vacancies in a three-state region in the far west. She filed application for five positions that were especially attractive to her. She was interviewed in three of these school districts and was offered two of the positions. One of the districts was located in the suburbs of a large California city with an enrollment of 13,400 students. The other had a much smaller enrollment of 3,100 pupils, but was highly attractive to Lorraine because of the nature of its community. After weighing the two opportunities, she chose the latter and became superintendent of the University Hills School District.

University Hills is a peaceful and prosperous community that serves as home to one of its state's largest universities. Nearly eight out of every ten of the adult residents in University Hills is a college graduate, making it the most "educated community" in the state. The public schools in University Hills have an outstanding reputation. About 85 percent of the high school graduates go on to four-year institutions of higher education.

The city and the school district have no room for growth. Virtually all of the available land has been developed in University Hills. With a declining birth rate (the fertility rate for females has dropped from 2.0 to 1.5 in the past fifteen years), the school system is experiencing declining enrollments. In 1975, there were 4,200 students in the district. Over the past fifteen years enrollment has declined 26 percent. One elementary school has been closed, leaving the district with three elementary schools, one middle school, and one high school.

There were numerous conditions that attracted Lorraine to University Hills. Among the more weighty were the following: (1) the parents placed an unusually high priority on elementary and secondary education; (2) the teaching and administrative salaries were among the highest in the state; (3) the schools and the university had developed a close working relationship; (4) the school distirct had a record of stability with regard to leadership (e.g., the superintendent she was replacing was retiring after holding the position for twenty-two years); and, (5) the school board consisted of well-educated citizens who did not appear to be on political missions. Additionally, Lorraine was impressed by the fact that an inordinate amount of time and effort was devoted to instructional improvement in this district. Teachers were employed to work on curriculum projects during the summer months, there was an ongoing staff development program with clear objectives, and the district had a comprehensive approach to program evaluation.

Dr. Lorraine Marcum arrived in University Hills on July 1 to assume her new position. She established three goals for the first week: (1) meet all of the administrative staff, (2) visit each of the schools, and (3) become familiar with statistical data concerning the district. With regard to the latter goal, she learned the following about the school system:

- the geographic size was only 9.3 square miles
- the school district owned only three buses (very few students were transported to and from school)
- the school district had one of the highest property taxes in the state
- there were no manufacturing operations in the school district; retail stores constituted the only source of taxable property other than private residences
- the per pupil expenditures ranked in the top 2 percent for the school districts in that state.

Lorraine also tried to learn more about the five school board members. She met each of them twice during her two interview visits to University Hills. The members included: *Board*

- Deloris Steck, housewife, president
- David Nicolet, biology professor
- Joel Silver, restaurant owner
- Marcia Pilko, music professor
- Elizabeth Jones, pediatrician

Mrs. Steck is married to the dean of the College of Arts and Sciences at the university, and Dr. Jones occasionally teaches courses in microbiology for the university. Thus, four of the five board members are linked to the university.

The central office administrative staff consists of John Oberdorf, assistant superintendent for business, and Vivian Smith, director of instructional programs. During the first month of the job, Lorraine met with the two frequently. It was during her meetings with John that she became aware of the financial difficulties facing the school district. At no time during her interviews was she told that the district was faced with funding problems. Lorraine realized that she did not ask questions about finances and the board did not volunteer information on this topic. Thus, the assistant superintendent's disclosures of financial difficulties came as a surprise and the news truly bothered the otherwise confident educational leader.

Lorraine is the first to admit that she is not very experienced when it comes to business administration. Her background is in instruction and curriculum. As a principal she had some contact with fiscal responsibilities, but these experiences were narrow in scope (e.g., activity funds, lunch funds). The problems described by the assistant superintendent for business were complex and Lorraine realized that she would need to rely heavily on him for counsel.

In a meeting several weeks before school is scheduled to open for fall semester, the superintendent and her administrative staff discuss the financial problems in relation to several initiatives. Lorraine opens the discussion with a summary of the problem.

"Mr. Oberdorf has convinced me that we cannot go on spending money as we have in the past. Our analysis indicates that we are in no position to institute two new programs scheduled to begin this fall, and we must cut $50,000 from our budget to remain in the black. The two new programs, as you know, are the employment of a half-time music teacher to initiate a strings program for the elementary schools and the addition of a second counselor for the elementary schools. Neither of the positions has been filled, although the recommendations for employing individuals have been sitting on my desk for over a week. Additionally, John has recommended that we cut $10,000 from staff travel and $40,000 from equipment purchases. Before taking this matter to the board, I wanted to hear what you had to say about these recommended actions. Your opinions are important to me."

Karen Holloway, an elementary principal, was the first to react to the superintendent. "Did John or Vivian talk to you about how these two new initiatives got approved?" she asked.

Before the superintendent could respond, the assistant superintendent for business intervened. "What difference does it make how the programs came about? We just can't afford them."

"I think it makes a tremendous difference," the principal answered. "The second counselor resulted from a two-year study of a teachers' committee. The strings program had a very different origin. A board member, Dr. Pilko, led a parent group that demanded that the program be offered. They spent two months passing petitions throughout the community and the board voted five to zero to institute the program this fall. There are going to be some angry board members and some angry parents if we don't offer strings in the elementary schools. I suppose the second counselor issue is less volatile; but nevertheless, there will be some teachers upset if we don't pursue it."

The assistant superintendent for business shot back, "Fine, let's make everyone happy. But what are we going to cut out? It's one thing to tell us what to offer but it's another to recommend to discontinue something."

It was obvious to all present that tension was building between the business official and the elementary principal. Karen Holloway is known as a fighter because she does not back away.

"Sure, I'll be happy to tell you what we should cut. Let's get rid of some of the athletic programs at the middle school and high school," Karen said. "That stuff is not as important as the two elementary programs we've been discussing."

At that point, Rich Dawson, the high school principal, looked up from the fall class schedule he was reviewing and joined the debate. "That's real smart, Karen. Getting rid of athletics is your answer to every problem. Don't you know that there are twice as many parents who would sign a petition for athletics as those who want a few children to learn to play the violin in third grade? Further, I support John's notion of where we should cut the $50,000. The district has to remain in decent financial shape."

Dr. Marcum decided she better intervene before war officially broke out. "Hold it, now. Let's not get into shouting matches. This is not an easy issue. If it were, we wouldn't be here discussing it. I have a few questions I would like answered. First, why is it, John, that the previous superintendent left these items in the budget if there weren't sufficient funds to pay for them?" she inquired.

"I told him when we prepared the budget that there was a problem. You've got to realize two things about your predecessor. He approached problems optimistically, believing that there were solutions out there even though he wasn't sure what they were. Second, he was retiring. He said the public and teachers wanted these programs and the new superintendent would have to deal with it," John answered.

"I'd like to hear what the rest of you have to say about all of this," Lorraine said looking at the three principals and the director of instruction who thus far had been silent in the meeting.

Norma Cosgrove, another elementary principal, indicated that she was in complete agreement with Karen Holloway. Not instituting the two new programs would be a political mistake.

Bart O'Malley, the middle school principal, suggested that the decision should not be made hastily. He recommended that a special study committee be formulated to examine the budget problems, and in the interim, no programs be added or cut.

Ron Dillis, the third elementary principal, and Vivian Smith, the director of instruction, both indicated they would go along with whatever the superintendent decided. They based their response on the belief that Dr. Marcum was the chief executive and their job was to support whatever decisions were made.

The comments by these individuals did little to mollify either Karen Holloway or Rich Dawson. Dawson managed to speak again before his adversary could regain the floor.

"Dr. Marcum, I think you ought to listen to John. He's been here a long time. We don't have time for study committees and we certainly don't want to engage in knee jerk reactions like cutting athletic programs," he said.

Karen responded immediately, "Again, Dr. Marcum, I implore you to look at the dynamics that led to these new programs for elementary schools. I'm not on a crusade to eliminate or curtail athletics. I was asked what was less important and should be cut, and I gave you my opinion. I think if you go forward and recommend not initiating these two programs, you will have been poorly advised by some of your staff. Believe me, the teachers and parents will be watching how you come down on this issue."

The superintendent could see that this matter would not be resolved in this meeting. Tempers were getting short and the comments were becoming less and less productive. She moved on to other agenda items and completed the meeting without resolving the issue of new programs. Later that afternoon she sat in her office and reviewed the positions taken by her staff:

- *Position A:* Do not institute the two new programs and cut $50,000 from staff travel and equipment purchases (supported by the assistant superintendent for business and the high school principal).
- *Position B:* Leave the new programs alone and eliminate athletic programs at the middle and high school to a level sufficient to cover projected deficits (supported by two elementary principals).
- *Position C:* Institute a special study committee and do not implement any new programs or cut any existing programs until study is completed (supported by the middle school principal).
- *Position D:* The superintendent should make the decision and all administrative staff should be supportive of that decision (supported by the director of instruction and one elementary principal).

With the last board meeting before the start of school only one week away, Lorraine perceived the differences among her staff to be indicative of the difficulty of the decision that she had to make. She mentally berated herself for not being more thorough in her questioning of the status of the district when she interviewed for the superintendency. She quickly realized that she had to turn her attention to more productive thoughts. She had to formulate a recommendation for the school board.

THE CHALLENGE: Place yourself in Dr. Marcum's position. What would you do in this situation?

KEY ISSUE/QUESTIONS:

1. Are the two elementary principals correct when they warn the superintendent that this is a politically explosive issue? What information in the case leads you to your conclusion on this question?
2. Identify the advantages and disadvantages of each of the positions advocated by members of the administrative staff.
3. If you were a principal in this district, what position would you take? Would it matter if you were an elementary, middle, or high school principal?

4. What is your assessment of the fact that Dr. Marcum knew nothing about financial difficulties until assuming the superintendency?

5. In what ways does the community environment make this case somewhat unique?

6. Is it important that one of the school board members was a leader in passing petitions to initiate the strings program?

7. In your opinion, what would occur if the superintendent decided to initiate the strings program but not add the second counselor?

8. Give your assessment of each of the administrators based on what is presented in this case. If you were a superintendent, would you want these individuals on your staff? Why or why not?

9. Given that this issue is being confronted during the first six weeks of the superintendent's tenure in the district, does the case have any special significance?

10. In your opinion, does Dr. Marcum have any advantages over her predecessor in addressing the financial woes of the district?

SUGGESTED READINGS:

Benson, N., & Malone, P. (1987). Teacher beliefs about shared decision making and work alienation. *Education, 107,* 244–251.

Cibulka, J. (1987). Theories of education budgeting: Lessons from management of decline. *Educational Administration Quarterly, 23*(4), 7–40.

Grandori, A. (1984). A prescriptive contingency view of organizational decision making. *Administrative Science Quarterly, 29,* 192–208.

Guthrie, J., & Reed, R. (1986). *Educational administration and policy,* pp. 241–245. Englewood Cliffs, NJ: Prentice-Hall.

Hoy, W., & Miskel, C. (1987). *Educational administration: Theory, research and practice* (3rd. ed.), pp. 332–350. New York: Random House.

Lakowski, G. (1987). Values and decision making in educational administration. *Educational Administration Quarterly, 23*(4), 70–82.

Lowe, R., & Gervails, R. (1987). How to handle desperation budget cuts without despair. *Executive Educator, 9*(1), 18–19.

Lyons, J. (1987). A study of public school principals' decision-making authority and autonomy. *Contemporary Education, 58*(4), 197–200.

Ornstein, A. (1989). Trimming the fat, stretching the meat for 1990s budgets. *The School Administrator, 9*(46), 20–21.

Owens, R., & Lewis, E. (1976). Managing participation in organizational decisions. *Group and Organizational Studies, 1,* 55–56.

Pajak, E. (1989). *The central office supervisor of curriculum and instruction,* chap. 12. Boston: Allyn & Bacon.

Parker, S. (1984). Cutting school budgets: Dangers and opportunities. *Contemporary Education, 55*(3), 160–163.

Poster, J. (1987). *The limits of consensus.* ERIC, Document Number ED280189.

Roetter, P. (1987). *Decision making style: Does it make a difference?* Unpublished Ph.D. thesis, University of Michigan, Ann Arbor.

CASE 7

Using Committees to Make Key Decisions

The "Not So Petty" Problem

THE COMMUNITY

Oxford County is located in a mid-Atlantic state. The county seat is Fullmer, a small city with about 45,000 residents. There has been some modest growth in the area due largely to the in-migration of retirees. The overall county population increased by 5 percent from 1980 to 1990. Senior citizens are attracted by the mild climate, scenic beauty, and the change of seasons (the county is just far enough north to maintain four distinctive seasons). These environmental factors are augmented by the relatively low cost of land, low property taxes, and a limited amount of industry.

Most counties in this state encourage industrial development as a means of economic growth. Executives of both foreign and domestic companies are courted by local officials. The development of industrial parks, enterprise zones, and tax abatement programs are rather common—but not in Oxford County. The Oxford Chamber of Commerce emphasizes tourism and promotes the development of retirement villas rather than manufacturing operations.

Several relatively small manufacturing companies are located in Fullmer, having been established more than fifty years ago. The managers of these operations have periodically expressed concerns about the negative attitudes of local officials toward industrial development. One of the companies, a candy factory, is currently examining relocating its plant in a neighboring county's modern industrial park. But such threats have had virtually no impact on county officials who continually point out that they do not want to change the ecology of the county.

Six years ago, a new hospital was erected in Fullmer offering modern medical care to the residents of the county. This structure enhanced leverage with regard to attracting developers of retirement villas. The hospital, costing more than $45 million, is considered one of the most modern in the state. The county planning board judges the development of retirement complexes to fall within the county's well-known values and beliefs concerning the protection of the scenic environment.

THE SCHOOL DISTRICT

The Oxford County School District is an all-county school system. It has a current enrollment of 21,500 students and operates the following attendance centers:

- two high schools, grades 9–12
- four middle schools, grades 6–8
- thirteen elementary schools, grades K–5
- a vocational school (also includes an alternative program for secondary students not enrolled in a regular high school program)

Enrollment in the school system has remained somewhat stable over the past decade; but in the last two years, kindergarten enrollments have declined by 7 percent.

The school district is governed by a seven-member school board; each member is elected to represent a specified geographic area within the county. There are nine townships in the county. The seats on the board are distributed as follows:

- Center Township (Fullmer)—2 seats
- Abington Township—1 seat
- Covington Township—1 seat
- Delaware and Potter Townships—1 seat
- Ealon and Mud Creek Townships—1 seat
- Richards and Washington Townships—1 seat

The central office staff in the district has remained very stable over the past ten years. The data below exhibit the positions and tenure of the administrators at the director and assistant superintendent levels:

Name	Position	Years in Position	Years in District
Bob Andrevet	assistant superintendent/ curriculum	8	24
Pamela Davis	assistant superintendent/ business	12	15
Jake Barnes	director/personnel	10	27
Neil Vickers	director/transportation	7	7
Iran Sults	director/maintenance	21	26
Anne Major	director/federal programs	9	16
Margo Jasik	director/special education	6	6

The superintendent, Dr. Rudy Quillen, is in his first year with the school district. He replaced Orville Cruthers who served as the chief executive of the Oxford County School District for 18 years.

THE INCIDENT

Dr. Quillen arrived in Oxford County in mid-July after having completed three years as superintendent of a much smaller district (2,400 students) in a neighboring state. Several of the board members in Oxford County met Dr. Quillen over a year ago at a national convention where he made a presentation on goal setting. They were so impressed with his presentation that they encouraged him to pursue the superintendent's job in their district when it formally became vacant. At age 38, Rudy Quillen was in good health, well-experienced (over twelve years of administrative experience), and eager to test his leadership ideas in a much larger school system.

One of the first controversies facing the new superintendent centered on the use of petty cash funds by principals. Increasingly, legal questions were being raised about the existence and use of such funds. These funds were employed by principals for emergency situations or the purchase of small items that had to be obtained in a timely fashion. State auditors periodically questioned their existence but they stopped short of recommending their abolition. The perpetuation of these funds was especially bothersome to Pamela Davis, the assistant superintendent for business. She occasionally raised the topic with Dr. Quillen, suggesting that as a new superintendent he was in an advantageous position to eradicate the funds.

In the school system where Dr. Quillen was previously employed, petty cash funds existed but had never generated controversy. The current conflict presented a novel challenge for the superintendent and he decided to seek both information and counsel. Unfortunately, telephone calls to the state accounting office, the state school boards association, and the state department of education failed to provide a conclusive answer. There was a great deal of ambiguity and disagreement concerning the legality and utility of petty cash funds.

The topic of petty cash funds was placed on the agenda of the November meeting of the administrative team, which consisted of principals and central office administrators. When Superintendent Quillen got to this item on the agenda, he outlined his perceptions of the problem based on criticisms and caveats he had received. The superintendent pointed out that even several school board members asked why the funds were necessary. Although Dr. Quillen expected disagreement on the topic, he was shocked at the level of emotional intensity generated by this issue. All of the principals, for example, made it abundantly clear that they opposed abolition of the funds. They were supported by Bob Andrevet, the assistant superintendent for curriculum. Pamela Davis, by contrast, stated that the funds served no useful purpose and their very existence created a management concern. The possibility of misuse, she believed, outweighed any real benefits.

"It's pretty obvious to me," the superintendent announced, "that we don't all agree on this matter."

Pamela Davis realized that she was the person who would have to explain petty cash funds to auditors. She also realized that she was in the minority among the administrative staff on this issue. She quickly responded to Dr. Quillen.

"There are complex issues involved here. There are some serious management questions surrounding this practice. It seems to me that we don't resolve this matter by holding an election. We need a detailed study of the issue."

The superintendent agreed this was an issue that should not be resolved simply by taking a straw vote. He supported the suggestion of a study.

"Petty cash funds have existed in this school district for years and years. I don't suppose it will do much harm to wait another few months while we examine all the dynamics of this issue. The question is, who is going to conduct the study?"

The assistant superintendent for business answered immediately, "This is a fiscal matter. The responsibility for completing the study rests with my office."

Rich Kizer, a high school principal, strongly disagreed. "Pamela, your position on this matter is well known. How could you objectively look at this issue? I recommend that Bob Andrevet be responsible for doing it. After all, the principals report to him. Isn't he in the best position to look at the use of petty cash funds?"

Skillfully, Dr. Quillen brought the debate regarding who would conduct the study to a close. He said he would take the matter under advisement and announce his decision at the next meeting of the administrative team in two weeks. In the interim, he invited all parties to send him recommendations and suggestions in writing.

The next council meeting was held approximately two weeks later. The entire administrative team anxiously awaited the superintendent's decision. Some of the more astute administrators recognized that the decision on this matter could be very revealing with regard to their new superintendent's management style. To no one's disappointment, Dr. Quillen placed the item of a study committee at the top of the agenda.

"I have looked at this matter carefully," the superintendent began. "First, let me say I am more convinced now than before that this issue should be thoroughly studied. If for no other reason, there are some contrasting perceptions and judgments about the need, legality, and effectiveness of petty cash funds. The comments I received over the past two weeks can be placed into two categories. One includes urgings that the study be headed by the assistant superintendent for curriculum. Not surprisingly the other position is that the study should be completed by the assistant superintendent for business. Thus, the two weeks did not produce any suggestions that were not presented at our last meeting. After mulling over this issue, I have decided that neither of these individuals will chair the study. Instead, I am putting together an ad hoc committee consisting of two teachers, a parent who is an accountant, a high school senior, a parent who is an attorney, and Ann Major (director of federal programs). Ann will serve as chair of the committee.

The group sat in silence. It was obvious they were caught off guard. One of the principals finally broke the silence by asking, "This isn't a joke is it?"

With a smile, Dr. Quillen answered the question, "No, it's no joke. Nor is it simply a way of avoiding taking sides. I truly believe that such a committee can do an objective job of looking at petty cash funds. Every person I named is a stakeholder in this school district. Each is affected by critical decisions we make, and collectively, their views are valuable to us. Yet, each is sufficiently detached from the issue so that objectivity is likely."

After the meeting, Pamela Davis visited Dr. Quillen in his office. She pleaded with the superintendent to rescind his decision to formulate this committee.

"There are two things that really bother me," she asserted. "First, I see this as a slap in the face. Fiscal matters should be handled by my office. Otherwise, why have an assistant superintendent for business? Second, you should realize that the principals will work overtime to convince the teachers, students, and probably the parents that their position on this matter is correct. By creating this committee, you have reduced an important management issue to a political argument. I'm the one who faces the auditors when they raise questions about petty cash funds. Sooner or later we're going to have something illegal come up as a result of using them."

The superintendent also received a visit from Bob Andrevet. He too was disappointed with the superintendent's decision. He warned, "Dr. Quillen, the principals are really upset about all of this. They believe—no, we believe—that Pamela just wants to broaden her control over the operations of our schools. Principals already have to go to her with hats in hands begging for money. If they lose their petty cash funds, she will have even more to say about how the principals manage their schools. Your idea of a committee scares the principals because they think the committee members will be unduly influenced by simple management judgments. The committee members do not understand school administration. They are apt to come down on the side of money management."

THE CHALLENGE: Place yourself in Dr. Quillen's shoes. What would you do at this point?

Is the real problem the petty cash fund?
Relationship to s.te based mgt?

KEY ISSUES/QUESTIONS:

1. Identify the range of options available to the superintendent at this point. What are the advantages and disadvantages of each?
2. Why do you think the assistant superintendents reacted so strongly in this matter? Do you believe that the organizational climate has anything to do with their reactions?
3. Some administrators might argue that Dr. Quillen should have attempted to reach a compromise between the two assistant superintendents so that they could have presented a united front to the principals. Do you agree that this would have been a better alternative than the one he pursued? Why or why not?
4. Are ad hoc committees effective? What are the strengths and weaknesses of this approach in dealing with problems?

5. Do you believe that the issue in question is serious enough for the superintendent to risk his working relationships with his top two assistants?

6. Identify some steps the superintendent can take to assure the board and professional staff that his idea of an ad hoc committee can work.

7. If your were a principal in this district, how would you interpret the superintendent's decision to use a committee? Does this decision provide insight into the new superintendent's leadership style?

8. Discuss the concept of project management. Does it have any relevance to this case?

9. In the early 1960s, research on *career bound versus place bound* administrators emerged in the literature. Does this research have any value in analyzing behaviors in this case?

SUGGESTED READINGS:

Black, J., & English, F. (1986). *What they don't tell you in schools of education about school administration,* chap. 1. Lancaster, PA: Technomic.

Byers, G. (1984). *Training school staffs in concepts of participatory management in the Fairfax County Public Schools: An evaluation study.* Unpublished Ed.D. thesis, Virginia Polytechnic Institute and State University.

Carlson, R. (1961). Succession and performance among school superintendents. *Administrative Science Quarterly, 6,* 210–227.

Crowson, R. (1987). The local school district superintendency: A puzzling role. *Educational Administration Quarterly, 23*(4), 49–69.

Greenhalgh, J. (1978). *Practitioner's guide to school business management,* chap. 2. Boston: Allyn & Bacon.

Hanson, E. (1985). *Educational administration and organizational behavior* (2nd ed.), pp. 294–306. Boston: Allyn & Bacon.

Hughes, L., & Ubben, G. (1984). *The elementary principal's handbook* (2nd ed.). pp. 304–309. Boston: Allyn & Bacon.

Lakowski, G. (1987). Values and decision making in educational administration. *Educational Administration Quarterly, 23*(4), 70–82.

McInerney, W. (1985). Participation in educational planning at the school district level. *Planning and Changing, 16,* 206–215.

Miklos, E. (1988). Administrator selection, career patterns, succession, and socialization. In N. Boyan (Ed.), *Handbook of research on educational administration,* pp. 53–76. White Plains, NY: Longman.

Owens, R., & Lewis, E. (1976). Managing participation in organizational decisions. *Group and Organizational Studies, 1,* 55–56.

Pajak, E. (1989). *The central office supervisor of curriculum and instruction,* chap. 8. Boston: Allyn & Bacon.

Roetter, P. (1987). *Decision making style: Does it make a difference.* Unpublished Ph.D. thesis, University of Michigan, Ann Arbor.

Watson, P. (1986). Effective task forces: Getting a quality product in minimum time. *Planning and Changing, 17,* 131–145.

Yukl, G. (1989). *Leadership in organizations* (2nd ed.). chap. 3. Englewood Cliffs, NJ: Prentice-Hall.

CASE 8

An Effort to Study School-based Management

Lora Mipps has been secretary to the superintendent of the Lewis Public Schools for thirty-one years. In that period, she has outlasted eight superintendents. She could not help but wonder as she listened to the shouting coming from the superintendent's office if number nine was just around the corner.

Dr. George Pisak arrived in Lewis, a quiet community of 18,000 located in the "sun belt," just fifteen months ago. He accepted the superintendency because he was looking for new challenges in his professional career. For the previous twelve years, he occupied the position of assistant superintendent for instruction in one of the larger school districts in the south. His two children had now finished college and were married. George and his wife, Estelle, thought a change of scenery would be good for both of them.

The Pisaks came to Lewis well aware of the history of the school system. The longest tenure of a superintendent in recent times was five years; and in the past six years, the school system has had three different superintendents. In part, the instability was due to constant changes on the school board. It seemed that in almost every election, incumbents were defeated.

When George was contacted by Ken Hollman, a former professor, about the job in Lewis, he initially indicated he was not interested in the position. Dr. Hollman was retained by the board to assist with the search for a new superintendent; after six weeks of receiving applications, the consultant made a second attempt to induce his former student to apply for the position. The two men met for lunch in the city where George was living. Dr. Hollman outlined six reasons why he thought George should pursue this opportunity:

Why take the job?

1. The school district desperately needed someone who could provide fresh leadership ideas. Of the four most recent superintendents, three were promoted from within the district. Each of these three eventually met with insurmountable problems as the composition of the school board changed.

2. The school board now realizes that the superintendent must be more than a mere manager. They want someone who can lead, especially in instructional areas.

3. The board recognizes the poor reputation of the district and is willing to pay a high salary to obtain the right superintendent.

4. The community of Lewis is divided from a socioeconomic standpoint. To a large degree, this fact is responsible for the frequency of shifts in school board composition and initiatives. The board is now controlled by upper-middle-class and middle-class residents who are willing to commit to long-range reforms.

5. After all the turmoil in the district, the climate is right for a superintendent to meet the high levels of success.

6. The board is willing to let the superintendent replace any and all of the current administrative staff if such decisions are deemed necessary.

George acknowledged that he and his wife were interested in relocating, preferably to a smaller city. He had not given much thought to becoming a superintendent. Dr. Hollman can be a very convincing individual; and given that he was George's mentor in graduate school, his influence was especially potent. Before their luncheon concluded, George agreed to submit his application.

After two interviews, George was offered the superintendency in Lewis. The board voted four to one to employ him. He received a three-year contract at a salary $20,000 greater than that paid to the previous superintendent. Billy Foster, the board member casting the negative vote, called the salary for the new superintendent "outrageous." The unhappy board member who also objected to the dismissal of Dr. Pisak's predecessor, told the local press, "We have families in Lewis who can't afford to feed their children. Yet, we take public money and pay a superintendent $85,000. The voters will have a chance to say how they feel during the next school board election."

5 member B1

The four board members who supported Dr. Pisak were most helpful in his first few months in Lewis. They worked very hard to offset the negative statements of the dissident fellow board member. They were particularly helpful in seeing that the new superintendent met many people in the community. He was invited to speak to service clubs, church groups, and just about every other type of gathering. In the north part of Lewis, the more affluent neighborhoods, his reception was warm and friendly. In the southern half of Lewis, "the other side of the tracks," his reception was mixed.

The first six months in Lewis convinced George that he was dealing with two very different communities. The school board was now controlled by the "north" faction and the patrons in the southern half of the school district resented it. George started exploring ideas that could create a greater sense of ownership for all taxpayers in the community. He became especially interested in a concept called *school-based management*. He visited Salt Lake City, Utah and Hammond, Indiana where two models of the concept had been instituted. Additionally, he contacted his friend, Dr. Hollman, who provided the names of several professors who were working with school-based management on a national basis. The superintendent conducted telephone interviews with these individuals and obtained additional insights and information.

Dr. Pisak first revealed his interest in school-based management to his administrative staff in a meeting some nine months after his arrival in Lewis. It was obvious that about one-half of the administrators had no idea what he was talking about. Of those who knew something about school-based management, most seemed concerned that the concept might be brought to their school system. The superintendent distributed copies of several journal articles detailing purposes and operational features of school-based management. He informed his administrative staff that the discussion of this topic would continue at their next meeting in two weeks.

Keeping his word, Dr. Pisak raised the topic of school-based management a second time. He asked the administrators to react to the articles he had distributed. A few favorable remarks were made; but for the most part, the administrators expressed skepticism. The superintendent then informed his staff that he intended to recommend a detailed feasibility study regarding the adoption of school-based management in Lewis. He asked for their reactions. Three of the eight elementary principals supported this study; four thought it was a bad idea and one indicated that he still did not know enough about the concept to voice an opinion. All three secondary principals opposed the study. The two assistant superintendents were divided on the issue. Dr. Pisak thanked his staff for their candor and indicated he would weigh their input in reaching a decision on the matter.

After discussing the issue with some influential and respected leaders in other school districts and after talking again to Dr. Hollman, Dr. Pisak decided to move forward with his recommendation. He prepared the following recommendation to be placed in the school board packets:

Lewis School Board Meeting:

Topic: Feasibility Study for the Implementation of School-based Management

Superintendent Recommendation: (a) The board authorize that Dr. Shirley Lowe and Dr. Paul Swartz, professors at the state university, be retained as consultants to assist the district in completing a feasibility study. Each consultant shall receive a fee of $8,000. (b) The board authorize the formation of a task force to oversee the feasibility study with the following composition: two administrative staff members (appointed by the superintendent); five teachers (appointed by the superintendent); one school board member (appointed by the board president); and five patrons (each board member making one appointment).

Background Information: The Lewis School District has experienced pronounced changes in school board membership. Frequently these changes have been accompanied by radical shifts in philosophy. I believe the socioeconomic divisions of the community are largely responsible for this pattern. The changes in school board membership also result in administrative changes, particularly in the superintendency. If stability is not achieved, it will be extremely difficult to engage in long-range planning and to initiate programs that will improve our schools. It is my opinion that we must find ways of letting parents and other taxpayers in all parts of our school system to have a greater voice in decisions.

School-based management is a concept that permits this to occur. By establishing school councils composed of all elements of the school/community (i.e., teachers, administrators, parents, students), we will hopefully gain the support of most patrons in moving forward with reforms. In fairness to my administrative staff, I should tell you that a majority is not enthusiastic about the study.

The feasibility study will generate data that will permit us to more closely examine the advantages and disadvantages of school-based management in our district. The study is not a decision-making process. We may well decide after looking at the data, that school-based management will not work here. I urge you to support the study so that we can make informed choices in the future. The study will be completed in six to eight months and will include attitude surveys of both staff and community.

The recommendation was distributed to board members, and the item was placed on the agenda for the regular board meeting that was to take place four days later. When the high school principal, Ernie Duggon, saw the agenda, he called all of the other principals and asked them to attend a meeting at his house that evening. Nine of the eleven principals attended. Duggon outlined his dismay that the new superintendent was moving ahead with this idea even though most administrators in the district were opposed to the study. A petition was developed urging the superintendent not to move forward with this matter. It read as follows:

As building level administrators in Lewis, we respectfully request that you reconsider your recommendation regarding a feasibility study for implementing school-based management in our district. We offer three fundamental reasons for our request:

(1) School-based management is a controversial movement that has not worked well in some communities. It diminishes the control of principals over their schools.

(2) Placing teachers and parents in positions where they can make major decisions will only generate more conflict in a community that has had more than its share over the past six years.

(3) The money and human resources that would be devoted to this study could be better utilized studying ways we can improve our existing curriculum.

We believe that we have been loyal to you. We have not opposed your ideas in the community, nor have we undermined any of your initiatives. The administrative staff in this district is overwhelmingly opposed to your idea of having a study. Won't you respect our viewpoint?

The petition was signed by all nine principals attending the meeting.

Upon receiving the petition, Dr. Pisak initiated some inquiries trying to find out who instigated the petition. His grapevine quickly revealed who was responsible. Mr. Duggon was summoned to the superintendent's office.

The meeting between the two was not pleasant. The superintendent accused the principal of being a troublemaker. The principal accused the superintendent of being insensitive to his staff's feelings. Soon the two were shouting at each other. Mrs.

Mipps, the secretary had heard such commotion before, and that is why she wondered if yet another superintendent was on his way out of Lewis.

THE CHALLENGE: Place yourself in Dr. Pisak's position. What would you do at this point?

KEY ISSUES/QUESTIONS:

1. Assess the judgments the superintendent is making about the nature of the community and the relationship between a socioeconomic polarization and problems in the school district.
2. Was it appropriate for Dr. Hollman to talk Dr. Pisak into applying for the superintendency in Lewis?
3. Should Dr. Pisak have asked the principals their opinion if there was a chance he would ignore what they said?
4. Identify the strengths and weaknesses of school-based management.
5. To what extent do environmental conditions (community) and organizational climate affect the implementation of school-based management?
6. Evaluate the behavior of the high school principal in this matter. Do you believe the rapid turnover rate of superintendents in the district affected his behavior? Could his behavior have been affected by the fact that this is Dr. Pisak's first superintendency?
7. Should the superintendent have had more discussions with the board and administration before deciding to recommend the feasibility study?
8. If you were a principal in this school district, would you have signed the petition to the superintendent? Why or why not?
9. Are there any conditions in the community and school district that suggest the superintendent was correct in moving quickly to recommend a feasibility study?
10. Given the information in this case, how do you believe the board will react if: (a) the superintendent moves forward with his recommendation in spite of the petition, or (b) he decides to withdraw the recommendation because of the petition?

SUGGESTED READINGS:

Beaudette, D. (1987). *School-based management: A typology and analysis of practices in two New Hampshire school districts.* Unpublished Ed.D. thesis, Boston University.

Black, J., & English, F. (1986). *What they don't tell you in schools of education about school administration,* pp. 15–17. Lancaster, PA: Technomics.

Caldwell, S., & Wood, F. (1988). School-based improvement—Are we ready? *Educational Leadership, 46*(2), 50–53.

Cawelti, G. (1989). The elements of site-based management. *Educational Leadership, 46*(8), 46.

Chapman, J. (1988). A new conception of the principalship: Decentralization, devolution, and the administration of Australian schools. In D. Griffiths, R. Stout, & P. Forsyth (Eds.), *Leaders for American schools,* pp. 429–438. Berkeley, CA: McCutchan.

David, J. (1989). Synthesis of research on school-based management. *Educational Leadership, 46*(8), 45–53.

Guthrie, J. (1986). School-based management: The next needed education reform. *Phi Delta Kappan, 68*(4), 305–309.

Guthrie, J., & Reed, R. (1986). *Educational administration and policy,* pp. 16–18. Englewood Cliffs, NJ: Prentice-Hall.

Hanson, E. (1985). *Educational administration and organizational behavior* (2nd ed.), pp. 76–78, 103–109. Boston: Allyn & Bacon.

Hoy, W., & Forsyth, P. (1986). *Effective supervision: Theory into practice,* pp. 168–177. New York: Random House.

Kowalski, T. (1986). The second coming of community education. *Contemporary Education, 57*(4), 194–197 (also in *Education Digest, 52*[6], 52–54).

Kowalski, T., & Fallon, J. (1986). *Community education: Processes and programs.* Fastback 243. Bloomington, IN: Phi Delta Kappa Educational Foundation.

Lawler, E. (1986). *High involvement management,* chap. 1. San Francisco: Jossey-Bass.

Lewis, A. (1989). *Restructuring American schools,* chap. 9. Arlington, VA: American Association of School Administrators.

McWalters, P. (1988). New realities call for new rules. *The School Administrator, 45*(8), 13–15.

Ratzki, A. (1988). Creating a school community: One model of how it can be done. *American Educator: The Professional Journal of the American Federation of Teachers, 12*(1), 10–17, 38–43.

Scarr, L. (1988). Lake Washington master plan: A system for growth. *Educational Leadership, 46*(2), 13–16.

Sergiovanni, T. (1987). *The principalship: A reflective practice perspective,* pp. 323–329. Boston: Allyn & Bacon.

Smith, J. (1985). *School based management.* Unpublished Ed.D. thesis, Harvard University.

Stover, D. (1989). But some principals feel threatened. *Executive Educator, 11*(1), 17.

Wicks, T., & Pankake, A. (1989–90). Board of education and superintendent: The team that "empowers" effectiveness. *National Forum of Educational Administration and Supervision Journal, 7*(1), 117–123.

Yukl, G. (1989). *Leadership in organizations* (2nd ed.), pp. 112–119. Englewood Cliffs, NJ: Prentice-Hall.

Zerchykov, R. (1985). Why school councils? *Equity and Choice, 2*(1), 37–38.

Involving Teachers
in Employment Decisions

THE COMMUNITY

Davidtown is located in the heart of farming country in a midwestern state. Unlike many similar towns, it has experienced steady growth through the 1970s and 1980s. In part, this growth is attributable to the following conditions: (1) Davidtown is a county seat; (2) it has a hospital that serves a four-county area; (3) it has a Chamber of Commerce that has been successful in bringing five new companies to the community in the last ten years; (4) it is located on a major interstate highway; and (5) it is the site of a public community college and a private four-year college.

The population of Davidtown is currently 24,300—a 40 percent increase in twenty years. New subdivisions are being erected continuously and a new shopping mall opened just three years ago. A recent fact book about the state described Davidtown as "a prosperous, growing, middle-class community."

A recent newspaper article highlighting community leaders noted that only one of five members of the city council had resided in Davidtown for more than ten years. This statistic exemplifies the changing demographics of the community. More importantly, it reflects the fact that leadership in Davidtown is composed largely of individuals who have recently located here.

THE SCHOOL DISTRICT

The boundaries for the Davidtown Community School District go beyond the town to include four rural townships. Thus, the student population of the school system still includes a number of students who live on farms. This fact is reflected in the composition of the school board:

- Joe Marshall, attorney (board president)
- Lisle Atwood, owner of farm implement dealership
- Mary Ingalls, bank employee
- Jim Maigthorn, farmer
- Lowell Ridovich, plant manager for a truck-trailer company
- Deloris Simpson, housewife and part-time instructor at the community college
- Byron Trumski, farmer

The board members representing the rural areas of the school district (Maigthorn and Trumski) are both serving their third terms on the board. The other board members are all serving their first term.

The district includes a high school, two middle schools, and eight elementary schools. Four of the elementary schools are located in Davidtown and the other four are dispersed in the four outlying townships. Six of the school buildings have been erected or remodeled in the past fifteen years.

Will Guyberger has been superintendent of the Davidtown Community Schools for seven years. Prior to this appointment, he was the principal of Davidtown High School for eight years. Superintendent Guyberger is considered a competent leader and has many supporters in the community. The assistant superintendent for business, Howard Grangal, has twenty-two years of experience in the district. However, Dr. Patricia McDowd, assistant superintendent for instruction, has been employed by the school system for only two years. It has only been in the past five or six years that the school system sought to recruit administrators from outside the system. This change in practice was prompted largely by demands made by new school board members who believed that the school district suffered from too much "inbreeding."

THE INCIDENT

For the first time since Will Guyberger left the principalship of Davidtown High School, the school was faced with the task of finding a new principal. Aaron Ketchie, who took over the principalship when Will Guyberger assumed the superintendency, was retiring.

Forty-seven educators filed applications to become principal of the high school. Included in the applicant pool were both assistant principals at the high school and the principal at the middle school. The task of coordinating the search for a new principal was delegated to the assistant superintendent for instruction, Dr. McDowd. Superintendent Guyberger believes in delegating responsibility and he does so often with his two assistant superintendents. Principals report directly to the assistant superintendent for instruction. Thus, assigning the responsibility for the search to Dr. McDowd was congruent with the existing line-and-staff relationships within the district.

Pat McDowd came to Davidtown from a neighboring state two years ago. The vacancy at the high school constituted the first opportunity she had to employ a principal. She viewed the situation as an opportunity to bring new ideas to the leadership of the school district. In commencing the search, Pat decided to advertise the position nationally in professional journals and newspapers—something that had never been done before in Davidtown. The publicity generated a large applicant pool.

In conducting the screening of the written materials submitted by the applicants, Pat conferred with both the superintendent and the assistant superintendent for business. She felt that both had a vested interest in this selection process, because they too would work closely with the individual. Although neither the superintendent nor the assistant superintendent for business campaigned directly for an individual candidate, it was apparent to Pat that they both favored employing someone from within the school system.

Six candidates were selected as finalists, including one of the assistant principals at the high school and the middle school principal. Each accepted the invitation to interview. The interviews were conducted by the two assistant superintendents and the superintendent. At her request, Pat's two colleagues completed evaluation forms for each candidate. After the interviews, two of the candidates withdrew from the search. One of the persons who withdrew was the middle school principal who felt he had little chance of getting the job. From the remaining four, Dr. McDowd recommended Dr. Sharon White, assistant principal at the laboratory school at the state university, for the job. She did so knowing that both of her central office colleagues favored the assistant principal at the high school. This was quite evident in their written assessments of the candidates completed after the interviews.

Superintendent Guyberger, however, believes that delegation of authority will only be successful if the superintendent is willing to permit subordinates to make critical decisions. Additionally, Will Guyberger was impressed with Dr. White, he just did not think she was any better than the internal candidate. After weighing the matter, he decided to take the recommendation to the school board.

Sharon White became the first female secondary school principal (two women hold posts as elementary school principals) and the youngest person (age thirty) to ever be appointed to a principalship in the Davidtown school district. She recently completed her doctorate in educational leadership and her two years of experience at the laboratory school constitute her total years of experience in school administration. Prior to becoming an assistant principal, Sharon taught English at a high school for five years.

The first semester at Davidtown High School was a successful and pleasant experience for the new principal. The faculty, students, and parents were quite impressed with Dr. White. Her pleasant personality and sincere enthusiasm made many skeptics forget about her youth. Even the two assistant principals who competed with her for the principalship became convinced that she was a most capable leader.

Sharon's style of leadership is distinctively different from that of her predecessor. She views herself as an instructional leader and devotes much of her time to interacting with teachers, students, and parents (e.g., visiting classrooms, attending virtually all of the extracurricular events). The management tasks were largely delegated to the two assistant principals; however, Dr. White maintained an active role in dealing with discipline problems.

In March, two faculty members at the high school indicated that they would not return for the following school year. On obtaining this information, Dr. White forwarded a study to her supervisor recommending approval to seek replacements and indicating the need for at least two additional positions for the coming school year due to anticipated enrollment increases. The superintendent reviewed the request and granted the authorization to fill all four positions.

Traditionally, principals in Davidtown have been given the authority to select teaching staff for their schools. Final decisions are subject to approval by the assistant superintendent for instruction and superintendent who also interview finalists for professional positions. The principal submits a recommendation to the assistant superintendent for instruction. She in turn checks with the assistant superintendent for business regarding funding, and the recommendation is forwarded to the superintendent for final approval and transmission to the school board.

In late April, Dr. White was in her office at the high school interviewing a candidate for a teaching position. A telephone call was received by her secretary from Superintendent Guyberger requesting a change in his time slot to interview the same candidate later in the day.

"Could you change my appointment with the math candidate today from 3:00 P.M. to 10:30 A.M.?" the superintendent inquired.

The secretary responded, "I don't think that's possible because the math department will be interviewing the candidate from 10:00 to 11:00 A.M."

There was a pause, and after collecting his thoughts the superintendent asked, "What is the math department doing interviewing candidates for teaching positions? I don't understand."

The secretary indicated that she did not know the answer and suggested that the superintendent ask the principal.

On ending his conversation with the secretary at the high school, the superintendent immediately called the assistant superintendent for business and asked him if he knew anything about teachers being involved in employment interviews at the high school. He often called Howard when he was in the dark about something, because his assistant had a reputation as one of the best informed persons in town. Howard said he knew nothing about it. He added a personal note,

"If this is occurring, it's a bad management decision." Next, Mr. Guyberger summoned his other assistant, Dr. McDowd, to his office.

"Did you know that Sharon White is involving teachers in the interviews for teaching vacancies at the high school?"

"No, she never discussed it with me," Dr. McDowd responded. "Are you sure? You really think the teachers are playing a formal role in the process?"

The superintendent shared his telephone conversation with his assistant and directed her to investigate the issue further and report back to him. It did not take long for Dr. McDowd to determine that Sharon White had indeed decided to let faculty play a role in the selection of new teachers. The principal based her decision to do so on two factors: (1) the time had come to recognize teacher empowerment, and (2) the process was used at the laboratory school where she previously was employed and it worked very well.

"Teachers need to have some input regarding who will be their professional peers. Physicians typically decide who gets to practice in a given hospital. Times are simply changing," explained the principal.

Dr. McDowd pointed out that the involvement of teachers in employment interviews was not an accepted practice in the school district.

"None of the principals is doing this except you. Mr. Guyberger is concerned about the possible repercussions. For example, will this involvement of teachers at the high school become an issue in collective bargaining? Will teachers demand that all principals use the same hiring practices? And how will the school board react when they find out about this? These are questions that bother us," explained the assistant superintendent.

Dr. White responded to these concerns, "I talked to the faculty about their roles in employing colleagues. They assure me that the involvement of teachers at the high school will not be used to try to force other schools in the district to do the same thing. Secondly, the recommendation for employment will still be mine. I take full responsibility for any recommendation that comes to your office."

"Did you ask your two assistant principals what they thought about involving teachers in hiring procedures?" the assistant superintendent inquired.

"Yes, we talked about it. They raised concerns privately with me but indicated that they thought the decision was mine. They did tell me that no other school in the system involved teachers in employment interviews. I work best when I have the confidence of my faculty. I trust them and they trust me. If you permit each principal to have latitude in employing faculty, why don't you trust my methods in reaching employment decisions?"

Dr. McDowd reported the conversation to the superintendent. She dwelled on the fact that the principal's decision could cause problems in negotiations with the teachers' union. The issue of faculty participation in employment interviews has been discussed at the bargaining table for at least the last three years, and in each instance, the board negotiator took the firm position that employment was a management responsibility.

"Sharon is being a bit naive if she thinks that the union is going to ignore this issue simply because some of her teachers told her it would not be used in collective bargaining," surmised the superintendent. "My guess is that they'll use it and point out that it was successful. They'll indicate that if teacher involvement doesn't work in another school, it's the principal's fault—certainly not the fault of the teachers. Our other principals are going to hit the ceiling when they find out about this."

The two officials discussed the issue for some time. They were joined by the assistant superintendent for business, Howard Grangle. Howard sits at the bargaining table with one of the school board members and the board's professional negotiator. Mr. Grangle suggested that they telephone the negotiator, an attorney named Roscoe Ferdinand, and get his opinion on the matter. Mr. Ferdinand was out of town for several days attending a workshop and was not available.

The superintendent's suspicions regarding the potential negative effects on collective bargaining received vigorous reinforcement from Howard Grangle. He urged the superintendent to take immediate action to stop the practice. Eventually the three central office administrators agreed that something had to be done. The two men favored sending a letter of reprimand to Dr. White. Such a letter could provide evidence that the involvement at the high school was not a practice condoned by the central administration. Dr. McDowd objected to sending a letter of reprimand. She thought the measure was too harsh. The superintendent decided to follow his own judgment and drafted the letter:

Dr. Sharon White:

In that you decided to involve your faculty in employment interviews without consulting with your supervisor, and in that this decision involved a matter of dispute between the Davidtown Teachers Association and the board of education, we find it necessary to issue this reprimand. This reprimand focuses solely on your judgments and actions in this matter. Issuing this letter is most difficult given that this problem is incongruent with your outstanding performance as principal over the last year. In the future, you should consult with the assistant superintendent for instruction and/or the superintendent on all decisions that have direct implication for either school board policy or negotiated agreements with the DTA.

W. Guyberger, superintendent

Dr. McDowd agreed that something had to be done, but she was bothered by the method being employed. She asked the superintendent if he would consider a conference with the principal as an alternative to informing her in writing that she could not continue the practice.

"No," answered the superintendent, "I think we have to go on record. I suggest you meet with Sharon and try to explain to her why this letter was necessary. She'll understand that it is not a reflection of the total job she is doing. After all, she is doing a very good job in all other areas."

THE CHALLENGE: Place yourself in Dr. White's position. What would you do at this point?

KEY ISSUES/QUESTIONS:

1. What options does Dr. White have at this point?
2. What alternatives could have been pursued by the superintendent and/or the assistant superintendent for instruction in dealing with this issue?
3. Identify conditions in the community that you believe are cogent to this case.
4. Identify conditions in the school district that you believe are cogent to this case.

5. Do you believe that the assistant superintendent for instruction should be held accountable for the decisions of the high school principal?
6. Describe what is meant by *teacher empowerment*. In general, do you agree with the principal's judgment that teacher empowerment is needed? Why or why not?
7. Evaluate the principal's position that she is responsible for employment recommendations and ought to be given the latitude to determine who will be involved in the interviewing process.
8. Assess the position taken by the two assistant principals in this case.
9. Suppose the principal had received a verbal rather than a written reprimand. Do you believe it would have had the same effect?

SUGGESTED READINGS:

Belasco, J., & Alutto, J. (1972). Decisional participation and teacher satisfaction. *Educational Administration Quarterly, 8*(1), 44–58.

Boyan, N. (1988). Describing and explaining administrative behavior. In N. Boyan (Ed.), *Handbook of research on educational administration*, pp. 77–97. White Plains, NY: Longman.

Bredeson, P. (1983). The secondary school principal's role in personnel screening and selection. *High School Journal, 67*, 6–10.

Bromert, J. (1984). The role and effectiveness of search committees. *AAHE Bulletin*, April, 7–10.

Castetter, W. (1985). *The personnel function in educational administration* (4th ed.), chap. 9. New York: Macmillan.

Conway, J. (1984). The myth, mystery, and mastery of participative decision making in education. *Educational Administration Quarterly, 20*(3), 11–40.

Ellis, T. et al. (1987). *Improving school effectiveness through reform of teacher selection practices and collegial observation of classroom performance.* ERIC, Document Number ED281902.

Lewis, A. (1989). *Restructuring America's schools*, chap. 4. Arlington, VA: American Association of School Administrators.

Macguire, J. (1983). Faculty participation in interviewing teacher candidates. *Clearing House, 56*(7), 330–331.

Maxwell, L. (1987). *Improving the selection of teachers: Research in brief.* ERIC, Document Number ED282850.

McPherson, R., & Crowson, R. (1987). Sources of constraints and opportunities for discretion in the principalship. In J. Lane & H. Waldberg (Eds.), *Effective school leadership: Policy and process.* pp. 129–156. Berkeley, CA: McCutchan.

Owens, R., & Lewis, E. (1976). Managing participation in organizational decisions. *Group and Organizational Studies, 1*, 56–66.

Pigford, A. (1989). How to hire teachers that fit. *The School Administrator, 10*(46), 38, 43.

Snyder, K., & Anderson, R. (1986). *Managing productive schools: Toward an ecology*, chap. 1. Orlando, FL: Academic Press College Division.

Snyder, P. (1985). *Perceptions of the managerial behavior of average and unusually effective high school principals.* Unpublished Ph.D. thesis, Pennsylvania State University.

Stuckwisch, D. (1986). *Patterns of participative decision-making: A study of high schools that promote decision sharing practices.* Unpublished Ph.D. thesis, Virginia Commonwealth University.

Tracy, S. (1986). *Finding the right person—and collegiality.* ERIC, Document Number EJ334581.

Tursman, C. (1989). Ways to fight teacher burnout: An interview with Ivan Fitzwater. *The School Administrator, 46*(3), 30, 35.

Zirkel, P., & Gluckman, I. (1986). Letters of reprimand: The important questions. *NASSP Bulletin, 70*(491), 99–102.

Restricting Employment
Opportunities

Keeping It In the Family

Fort Jason is located in a remote area of a southwestern state. The town itself is quite small, with only about 1,200 residents. The main street is lined with buildings erected in the 1920s and 1930s. Visitors who stroll through Fort Jason get the feeling that they stepped into a time machine and have been sent back to the 1950s. There's still a red and white twirling pole in front of the barber shop, the drug store still has a soda fountain, and the convenience store is still called the "five and ten."

The nicest building on Main Street is the Fort Jason Bank. The bank as well as the building are owned by the Quince family. Some residents contend that the Quince family owns most of the buildings in the small downtown area. Lucius Quince started the bank some fifty years ago, and when he passed away he left the business and other properties to his three sons. Donny Quince operates the family ranch in Fort Jason; David Quince is a state senator and practices dentistry in Fort Jason; and brother Jimmy runs the bank.

Many of the residents in Fort Jason are employed in Grundy, a city of about 18,500 located twenty-seven miles away. The largest employers in Fort Jason, per se, are the school system, the bank, and a jewelry company. The jewelry company employs about forty persons.

In towns like Fort Jason, the public school system is an entity that touches the lives of most citizens. Virtually everyone who resides here either has children in the school system or a relative that works for the school system. The high school football team is a source of community pride. Twice in the last five years, the Fort Jason Mustangs made it to the state finals for small enrollment high schools.

The school district is governed by a five-member board. Members are elected to three-year terms. The president of the board for the past nine years has been Jimmy Quince. Other members include:

- Lila Thims, housewife
- Bert Olsen, manager at the jewelry factory
- Andy Langston, bank employee
- Carl Davis, carpenter who works in Grundy

Last year the school board was faced with the task of hiring a new superintendent to replace LeRoy Weaver, who had retired and moved away. They selected Victor Miers, a principal at a boarding school operated by the U.S. Bureau of Indian Affairs. Victor's aunt lives in Fort Jason and wrote him about the position when it became vacant. Being a successful principal and still relatively young at thirty-eight years old, Victor viewed the job in Fort Jason as an opportunity for professional growth.

From the very first moment Victor met the school board in his job interview, it was abundantly clear that Jimmy Quince was in charge of the school district. The other board members treated him with reverence and he was not bashful about letting them know what he wanted. Mr. Quince dominated the interview. Two of the board members never even asked a question. The board interviewed three candidates for the position, and Jimmy Quince did not like two of them. Victor got the job.

Victor occupied his new office on July 1. To no one's surprise, Jimmy Quince was the first person to visit him in his office. The two had a straightforward conversation that consumed much of the afternoon.

"This is a good place to live and work," the board president commented. "Our last superintendent was here fifteen years. He knew how to do things right. He didn't start any trouble and he didn't have all these foolish ideas many educators have today. Fort Jason is full of good people; honest people who just want their children to receive a good basic education."

Victor realized that being superintendent in the small rural district was not the easiest job in the world. He remembered his professors sharing stories of how politics in small and rural districts could be just as intense as they often were in urban settings. Yet, compared to his last administrative job, Victor thought he had died and gone to heaven.

There are only two school buildings in the district. The elementary school houses grades kindergarten through six and the junior/senior high school houses grades seven through twelve. One of the earliest judgments that the new superintendent made was that employees were not apt to be a problem. The teachers and principals in this district follow orders. Victor had never worked with individuals who were more accommodating.

During the first few months of his tenure, Victor was not surprised to learn that Jimmy Quince took an active role in running the school district. A week never went by without the board president visiting a school or coming to the superintendent's office. Jimmy's visits with the superintendent ranged from sharing recommendations for purchasing school bus tires to ideas about good teaching. Jimmy liked Victor and he tried to help him adjust to his new position; but he never let the superintendent forget who was in charge.

Very few employees resign from the school district. The vast majority stay until retirement, especially the custodians, bus drivers, cooks, and secretaries. With jobs so scarce in Fort Jason, these positions are considered quite valuable. Additionally, the school district has historically employed residents of the community. Thus, many were not anxious to relocate. Victor recognized this fact as he prepared the agenda for the April board meeting. The announcement that the school district would be replacing a retiring custodian and secretary the following year was sure to cause many local residents to inquire.

When the board members received their packets three days prior to the meeting, they found the following item included:

Personnel Matter: Need to Replace Custodian at Jr./Sr. High School and Secretary at the Elementary School due to two retirements.

Action: The superintendent will place ads in the newspapers in Grundy and Fort Jason (the latter is published just once per week) and the vacancies will be posted in each of the schools.

After reading this item, Jimmy Quince called the superintendent and insisted on an appointment that afternoon. When he arrived at the superintendent's office, the board president got directly to the matter on his mind.

"What's this about placing ads in the paper in Grundy for a secretary and custodian? Why do we need to do that?" Mr. Quince inquired.

"I thought that it would get us a better applicant pool," Victor responded. "Additionally, there might be some people here in Fort Jason who will read about the vacancies in the Grundy paper. The paper here doesn't come out everyday, and I just took for granted that most people here subscribe to the Grundy paper."

"Victor, you don't have to worry about people in town here finding out about these positions. Once we announce them at the board meeting this week, the news will be all over town. Placing an ad in the Grundy paper will only get us some applications we don't want to consider."

The superintendent looked puzzled and asked, "What do you mean by applications we don't want to consider? I don't understand."

"Look," responded the banker, "we need to look out for folks in our town. We're not going to be providing jobs for taxpayers in Grundy. We owe it to the folks here to let them have first crack at vacancies in our school district. If we don't get a sufficient number of applicants from here, and I know that won't occur, then we can talk about placing an ad in the Grundy paper."

"Are you saying that we have to give preference to local taxpayers for jobs in our school district?" asked the superintendent.

"Damn right. That's exactly what I'm saying. These folks in Fort Jason work hard to support our schools. Why should we give the jobs to someone who doesn't even live here?"

"I've always believed," answered the superintendent, "that you hire the best individual you can find. We should be concerned with the person's qualifications, not where he or she lives."

"Come on, Victor, I'm not telling you to hire unqualified people. I'm just saying that we need to take care of our citizens first. In fact, we don't need to place any ads. Let's just post the vacancies in our schools and here in your office. Why the five board members alone can come up with a list of job applicants as long as your arm. Why, Lila Thims's son is looking for a job. He'd make a good custodian."

The more Victor listened to his board president, the more concerned he became. Thoughts about legal and ethical questions popped into his mind. Could the school district get by without advertising the positions? What if someone questioned the employment practices in the school district? Victor knows that his role is to be the professional leader of the school district. He is the person that is expected to provide leadership for the school board. He tried once more to communicate with his board president.

"Mr. Quince, I think we ought to talk to our school attorney about this matter. I'm a little nervous about restricting our search to persons who live in the school district. I'm not sure we can do that."

The board president looked directly into the eyes of the superintendent and said, "Listen, I'm sure we can do it. I'm sure we've been doing it. And, I'm sure we're going to continue doing it. Why, there are school systems in big cities that make employees live in the district. So why can't we employ our own taxpayers. Again, I want to point out that we're not talking about hiring unqualified people. But we have to give our own folks a chance. Look Victor, I have to get back to the bank. You forget about these ads and everything will be fine. Anybody gives you trouble, you send them to see me. I'll take care of it. Trust me."

As the board president left the office, Victor slumped in his chair. He looked out the window and agonized over what he should do.

THE CHALLENGE: Assume the position of the superintendent. What would you do?

KEY ISSUES/QUESTIONS:

1. What alternatives does the superintendent have in this matter?
2. What are the advantages and disadvantages of the superintendent simply agreeing to do what the board president desires?
3. What legal issue are raised in this case?
4. Why do you believe that Jimmy Quince has been president of the school board for so long?
5. What are the advantages and disadvantages of having very little turnover in membership on a school board?
6. Do some school districts require employees to live within the school district? Beyond legal questions, do you believe a residency requirement is a good policy?
7. What inferences can be drawn from the behavior of the school board president in this case?

8. What reactions could be expected if the superintendent decides to talk to each board member individually about this problem?

9. Is this case important enough for the superintendent to make a major issue out of it?

SUGGESTED READINGS:

Black, J., & English, F. (1986). *What they don't tell you in schools of education about school administration*, pp. 46–49. Lancaster, PA: Technomic.

Castetter, W. (1985). *The personnel function in educational administration* (4th ed.), chap. 9. New York: Macmillan.

Castetter, W. (1985/86). The personnel function: Coming of age. *National Forum of Educational Administration and Supervision, 2*(3), 18–24.

Darling, J., & Ishler, R. (1989/90). Strategic conflict management: A problem-oriented approach. *National Forum of Educational Administration and Supervision Journal, 7*(1), 87–103.

Good, F. (1987). *The role of the small school district superintendent as perceived by school board presidents, superintendents, and principals in selected California school districts.* Unpublished Ed.D. thesis, University of Southern California.

Guthrie, J., & Reed, R. (1986). Educational administration and policy, pp. 48–55. Englewood Cliffs, NJ: Prentice-Hall.

Institute for Educational Leadership (1986). *School boards: Strengthening grass roots leadership,* chap. 2. Washington, DC: Institute for Educational Leadership.

Kowalski, T. (1989). *Planning and managing school facilities,* pp. 142–144, 151–155. New York: Praeger.

Litman, J. (1987). *Perceptions of Indiana board of education members and superintendents on the separation of leadership responsibilities.* Unpublished Ed.D. thesis, Indiana University, Bloomington.

McDaniel, T. (1986). Learn these rarely written rules of effective board service. *American School Board Journal, 173*(5), 32.

McNamee, M. (1980). Tips on being an effective board president. *American School Board Journal, 167*(7), 17.

Murray, B. (1986). *The performance of Indiana school boards: A comparative study between the performance of Indiana school boards and the Indiana School Board Association guidelines as perceived by Indiana school superintendents.* Unpublished Ph.D. thesis, Indiana State University.

Sergiovanni, T., Burlingame, M., Coombs, F., & Thurston, P. (1987). *Educational governance and administration* (2nd ed.), pp. 210–216. Englewood Cliffs, NJ: Prentice-Hall.

Weber, J. (1986). *Community politics and the school superintendent.* Unpublished Ed.D. thesis, Teachers College, Columbia University.

Yukl, G. (1989). *Leadership in organizations* (2nd ed.), pp. 18–21, 34–36. Englewood Cliffs, NJ: Prentice-Hall.

The Closed Door Policy

The Boss A'nt In

THE COMMUNITY

Placid Falls is a suburban community that was developed in the early 1950s. Today, it is a well-established and well-known area approximately thirty-five miles from New York City. The residents are definitely upper middle class. Houses in the community are in the $300,000+ bracket. The 7,600 residents of this suburb take great pride in their community. Historically, they have been especially proud of their public schools.

The town of Placid Falls is governed by a five-member council. The mayor serves as chief executive officer of the board; however, the position is part-time. The current mayor is Dr. Samuel Halcowitz, a retired physician. The issues that come before the town council are rather routine, management issues that typically are not very controversial. The homogeniety of the community from an economic standpoint helps to reduce conflict situations that often arise in less mature suburbs. Occasionally the council will have to wrestle with a zoning question, but that is about as controversial as issues get in municipal government in Placid Falls. There is virtually no room left for development within the town boundaries. There are a few privately owned businesses in the community, most are fashionable clothing shops or chic restaurants.

THE SCHOOL SYSTEM

The Placid Falls Public School District consists of only four schools: two elementary schools (grades K–5); a middle school (grades 6–8); and a high school (grades 9–12). The total enrollment in the school district is 1,900. Enrollments have declined very slightly in the past decade, about 3 percent.

Approximately 90 percent of the graduates of the high school go on to four-year institutions of higher learning. About one-third of the graduating class will enroll in highly selective, prestigious colleges and universities. Thus academic competition in the schools, especially at the high school, is intense. Academic programs are stressed and very few students ever opt to take vocational courses (most of which have to be taken at an area vocational school).

The faculty and administration in the district are considered to be excellent, both by the residents and by the state department of education. Nearly 15 percent of the teachers and 75 percent of the administrators have doctorates. Salaries (among the highest in the state) are largely responsible for attracting outstanding educators to Placid Falls. Per pupil expenditures rank in the top 3 percent for school districts in the state.

THE ADMINISTRATION

Three years ago when the superintendency in Placid Falls was vacant, 123 candidates applied. The quality of the applicant pool was more important than the quantity of the candidates. Dr. George Frieman of Northwestern University was retained by the school board to assist with the search. A placement consultant with a national reputation, he did not disappoint the Placid Falls school board. The ten candidates interviewed by the school board included some of the best known superintendents in the United States. The successful candidate turned out to be Dr. Andrew Sagossi, a superintendent of a large county school system in North Carolina. He signed a four-year contract at a salary of $113,000 per year to become the new chief executive of Placid Falls.

Leaving a school district of 35,000 students to move to a school district of less than 2,000 students may be difficult to understand for most upwardly mobile administrators. But a closer examination of the facts reveals why Dr. Sagossi made this career move. First of all, he received a salary increase of $20,000. Moreover, he was interested in returning to the New York area where he was reared and where a number of relatives still resided. As he explained to the school board when he interviewed, "I have been superintendent in several school systems. I am no longer interested in trying to judge my career by the size of the organization. The quality of the work experience is now much more important to me. In a community such as Placid Falls, the superintendent has a much greater opportunity to work with community and state leaders to coordinate the efforts of the local schools."

At the time of Dr. Sagossi's appointment, the administrative staff in the district included the following individuals:

- Joan Myers, assistant superintendent for curriculum
- Al Yanko, assistant superintendent for administration

- Neil Larson, high school principal
- Joe O'Bannion, middle school principal
- Wilma Tucko and Andrea Kline, elementary principals

All are experienced leaders. The newest member of this administrative team is Dr. Myers.

Joan Myers was born and raised near Newark, New Jersey. She is the oldest of three children. Her father is a retired dentist and her mother recently retired as a marketing executive for a large department store. Her upper-middle-class homelife offered many cultural and educational opportunities. As an undergraduate, Joan attended a prestigious liberal arts college in New England. It was during her sophomore year that she decided to major in social science education. Her parents were more than a little disappointed by her career choice. They had hoped that she would enter medicine or dentistry.

While teaching for six years in a high school in Pennsylvania, Joan was able to finish her master's degree in school administration in Philadelphia. The graduate degree opened new doors for her and she accepted a position as an assistant principal in a large high school in western New York state. After just two years in this administrative position, Joan resigned to accept a doctoral fellowship that permitted her to continue her graduate studies on a full-time basis. The two and one-half years of doctoral study were exciting and enjoyable. Joan met and married Robert, a practicing attorney who was teaching part-time at the university's law school. After completing her doctorate in education, Joan looked for positions that were relatively close to New York City to accommodate her husband's affiliation with a large law firm there.

The position at Placid Falls was almost too good to be true. When Joan first saw the vacancy, she was reluctant to apply. With only two years of administrative experience as an assistant principal, she did not think she could be competitive for the job. She applied anyway. Her interview with the school district proved to be a smashing success. When she was offered the position, Joan felt like a student who just skipped two grade levels in school. She was in a position that she envisioned to be a part of her career some ten years down the road. She became the youngest administrator in Placid Falls—and the least experienced.

THE PROBLEM

Joan Myers has many strengths. Among the more obvious are her outgoing personality and her ability to motivate those around her. She generates an excitement about education. Although her title in the school system is "assistant superintendent," basically she is a staff administrator. That is, she does not have line authority for the principals. She works with administrators and teachers in a support and advisory capacity.

During the first four months in Placid Falls, Dr. Myers had very little contact with her boss, Dr. Sagossi. In fact, she noticed that the superintendent was not the type to spend much time in his office. While discussing a budget for a staff development project with the other assistant superintendent, Dr. Yanko, Joan mentioned that she did not have much opportunity to talk to Dr. Sagossi.

"Andy's not around very much," her colleague told her. "That doesn't mean he isn't putting in his time with the school district. He's the type of leader who believes in building community support and being active in professional organizations. He is very involved in state and national organizations. In fact, I think he has ambitions of pursuing the presidency of our state superintendents' association. He was president of the state superintendent's association in another state, and I think he liked the experience. You'll find that he leaves the operation of the school district pretty much to us."

Compared to the two other school districts where Joan had worked, Placid Falls seemed to be utopia. The superintendent could spend so much time away from his office because there just did not seem to be many of those natty problems that plagued most other public school systems. Employees were happy to be there; salaries were among the highest in the metropolitan area; and given the size of the school district, there were ample professional employees to assure that no one was overburdened.

In December, Joan attended a national conference on gifted and talented education. At the meeting she met Maggie Zorich, a program officer with a midwestern foundation. Maggie's attendance at the conference was related to six school districts that were receiving support from the foundation to conduct research relative to mentoring projects for middle grade students. The two sat next to each other at a luncheon, and Joan learned that Maggie was looking for several more school districts that might be interested in joining the project.

"Exactly how is the mentoring program structured?" Joan asked the foundation official.

"The primary purpose is to examine the benefits of taking students in the sixth grade and linking them with mentors for specialized study for two years," Maggie answered. "The mentors are usually persons in the community such as government officials, business leaders, physicians, engineers, and lawyers. The students are expected to spend approximately three hours per week working with the mentor on an approved project. We are interested in determining what effect such a program has on very bright children. For example, will this mentoring experience affect curricular choices later in high school? Will it affect career choices?"

Maggie invited Joan to submit a proposal to the foundation. Joan was very excited about the prospect of instituting a mentoring program in Placid Falls. The only difficulty she could see in doing so related to the specified time parameters. Due to funding cycles of the foundation, Joan had to prepare and submit the proposal in less than five weeks.

When Joan returned from the conference, she outlined what needed to be done to complete the proposal. First, she had to talk to the middle school principal to be sure that he was interested and would cooperate. Second, she had to determine a method for selecting students to participate in the program. Third, she had to build a pool of prospective mentors. Fourth, she had to identify a consultant who would conduct the research portion of the project (the foundation required that the investigator be a person not employed by the school district). Her final major task was to get Dr. Sagossi to agree to provide $30,000 in matching funding for the project. The first four tasks were accomplished with little difficulty, the final one proved to be more cumbersome.

The first day back from the conference, December 7, Joan walked across the hall to Dr. Sagossi's office in hopes of talking with him about the project proposal. Miss Halston, his secretary, told her that the superintendent was out of town at a conference and would not return until December 12. Joan then went to see Dr. Yanko, the administrator who controlled the budget. She explained the proposal and asked if he could approve the $30,000 needed for the school district's share of the funding.

"Only the boss and the school board can approve that kind of expenditure," Dr. Yanko told her. "Proposals for outside funding must be approved by the school board before they are submitted to funding agencies. And as you know, nothing goes to the school board for consideration unless Dr. Sagossi has reviewed the material and decides to make a positive recommendation. When do you have to submit this?"

"I think the last date is January 12." Joan replied.

"Well you still have the January board meeting. Let's see, the first Wednesday in January is the 3rd. You'll be okay."

After the conversation with her colleague, Joan went to see Miss Halston again to try to get an appointment with the superintendent when he returned from his conference. The secretary scheduled a meeting for 10:00 A.M. on December 13. She explained that December 12 would not be possible because the superintendent did not accept appointments on the first day he returned to the office after being out of town for more than one day.

Joan continued working on the proposal. In a way she thought the delay in seeing the superintendent could be beneficial because her work on the project would be nearly completed by the time she met with him. This would permit her to discuss the initiative in great detail. Joan saw Dr. Sagossi briefly on Wednesday the 12th, the day he returned to Placid Falls. The two exchanged greetings in the hallway of the administrative office, but there was no additional conversation. The following morning, there was an administrative staff meeting at 8:00 A.M. Such meetings were held only when Dr. Sagossi determined they were necessary. The meeting on December 13 was devoted to a series of reports the superintendent wanted to share with the administrative team. Dr. Sagossi also announced his plans to seek the presidency of the state superintendents' association. No one present was surprised. The meeting ended at approximately 9:30 A.M. At promptly 9:55 A.M., Joan arrived at Dr. Sagossi's office for her 10:00 A.M. appointment.

Miss Halston said, "I was just getting ready to call you. I'm afraid I'm going to have to change your appointment. Dr. Sagossi just received a telephone call that his mother is quite ill. He said he will be back in the office on Monday and he recommended that you should try to meet with him sometime that morning. His calendar is pretty clear and I'm sure he'll be able to chat with you then."

On Monday morning about 9:00 A.M., Joan tried once again to see the superintendent. This time Miss Halston told her that the board president was with the superintendent and that she did not know how long they would be together. Joan reminded the secretary that Dr. Sagossi was supposed to be able to see her and asked that she be summoned when the two men were finished with their conference.

At about 10:30 A.M., Miss Halston called Dr. Myers and apologized on behalf of the superintendent. Joan was told that a problem had surfaced and that it would be necessary to schedule an appointment for the next day. Joan looked at her calendar and realized that she had to go to a meeting regarding textbook adoptions in the state capital on Tuesday.

"How about Wednesday?" asked Joan. "Is he available on Wednesday?"

"No," the secretary answered. "He is scheduled to be at the university for an alumni advisory board meeting all that day. He will be back on Thursday."

At this point, Joan was becoming both frustrated and angry. She told Miss Halston, "Look, this is important. This is not that big an organization. I find it difficult to understand why I can't arrange to see the superintendent for just thirty minutes. There are thousands of dollars at stake, not to mention an excellent educational opportunity. I'm sure that if Dr. Sagossi knew why I wanted to see him, he would find the time."

"Dr. Myers," replied the secretary, "I don't make the rules. I just do my job. Let me talk to Dr. Sagossi to see if he can see you before the end of the week."

Fifteen minutes later the secretary called back and informed Dr. Myers that she should talk to Dr. Yanko about the matter.

"Tell Dr. Sagossi that I have already done that and he told me I had to talk to the superintendent," Joan impatiently responded. "Tell him I will send him something in writing and perhaps he can respond after he reads it."

After putting down the telephone, Joan realized that school would be dismissing for the holiday break in just four days. Furthermore, she realized that the agenda for the January 3rd board meeting was already being prepared. Joan went to the superintendent's office to see when board materials would be distributed for the January 3rd meeting. The secretary informed her that the packets, including the agenda, would be distributed one week before the meeting as always. Dr. Sagossi was going on vacation to Florida for ten days commencing on December 23, so he intended to complete the board packets by the afternoon of Friday, December 22. Once again, Dr. Myers pleaded her case, indicating that it was extremely important to see the superintendent about the grant proposal. Again she was told that she would have to make an appointment.

"Look, the only possible date left is Thursday, December 21. What if something else comes up and he cancels the appointment again?" Joan asked.

The secretary looked at Joan and said slowly, "Dr. Sagossi is a busy person. You cannot expect that he will see you whenever you like. If you have deadlines on a grant proposal, you should have talked to him about it weeks ago."

Dejected, Joan walked back to her office.

CASE 12

Captain Punishment

Rogers Middle School is located in a major city in a southwestern state. The school came into existence seven years ago as a result of population growth. The major portion of the students attending the school live in modest to low-cost housing erected over the past two decades. The Rogers facility is attractive and well-maintained, and it has become a source of pride for many families in the neighborhoods surrounding it.

The student population at Rogers mirrors the general population of this growing metropolitan area. Many of the students are bilingual. A recent study found that fourteen different languages are spoken by boys and girls who attend the school. The statistical report prepared for the central administration of the school system identifies the following breakdown of enrollment:

- Hispanic—41 percent
- Black—15 percent
- Caucasian—24 percent
- Native American—9 percent
- Indochinese—9 percent
- Other—2 percent

The staff at the school is less diverse. About two-thirds of the teachers, counselors, and administrators are caucasian.

Rogers Middle School contains grades six, seven, and eight. The total enrollment of the school is 1,150, and the capacity to absorb additional students is about exhausted. When the school first opened, it enrolled just over 700 pupils; the school has increased in enrollment every year since that time.

Within the total school system, Rogers is recognized as a model school. The students do relatively well on standardized tests, the school excels in extracurricular activities, and there are fewer suspensions and expulsions than at other middle schools in the district. Much of the credit for these accomplishments is attributed to the principal, Pete Sanchez.

Ever since he was an elementary school student in southern New Mexico, Pete Sanchez wanted to be a teacher. One of nine children, he found it impossible to attend college after graduating from high school. Like his siblings, he went to work in a local factory when he was eighteen years old. But Pete is not one who is easily discouraged. Over a span of seven years, he drove forty-five miles twice a week to take night classes at a state university. After finishing his first three years of college in this fashion, he quit his job in the factory, received a student loan, and finished his senior year as a full-time student. Not having to work and go to school simultaneously, he made all "As," including an "A" in student teaching.

Several of Pete's professors encouraged him to go on to graduate school. But being recently married and with a pregnant wife, he took a teaching position in a neighboring state. In addition to teaching high school mathematics, Pete assumed coaching duties. He was both the assistant football coach and the track coach. During a twelve-year tenure at this high school, he completed his master's degree and obtained certification as a secondary school principal. The first year after he received his administrative license, he was named an assistant principal at another school in the distrct. It was in this role as assistant principal that Pete first earned the title of "Captain Punishment."

During his three-year stint as an assistant principal, and during his tenure as principal of Rogers Middle School, Pete practiced a no nonsense approach to student discipline. In large measure his philosophy for dealing with problem students stemmed from his observation that many of the students at Rogers lacked proper guidance and discipline outside of school. This philosophy of dealing with pupil conduct included using his walnut paddle, which he dubbed "the board of education."

Rogers Middle School has one of the most active parent groups of all the schools in the district—and that includes elementary schools. Pete Sanchez spends a great deal of time with a number of parent committees he established in the seven years that Rogers has been in existence. He has been very skillful in involving parents in the activities of the school. He once told his immediate supervisor, Dr. Penelope Mackee, "When you have so many children coming from one-parent families, it is important to get that one parent involved in the school."

One of these committees focused on student discipline. It consisted of seven parents and three teachers. The issue of corporal punishment has been brought up several times over the years. Each time it emerged, Pete articulated his beliefs and outlined his purposes with regard to using a paddle and linked the discipline program to the overall success of the school. Repeatedly, the committee gave him near unanimous support to continue his tough approach to dealing with students who violated the rules of the school. Neither parents nor central office administrators criticized or challenged Mr. Sanchez's use of corporal punishment. In fact, a city newspaper and television station did special stories focusing on his image as a stern disciplinarian. Captain Punishment became somewhat of a hero. One mother interviewed for the television segment said. "Mr. Sanchez understands my children. He teaches them that they have to obey rules. Without a father at home, it is important that they receive added direction at school. I don't want the principal to be a nice guy who tries to be friends with my kids."

The faculty had mixed reactions to Mr. Sanchez's approach to dealing with students. The public image of the principal, however, dissuaded most of those who opposed his methods to speak out. Aaron Carson, a social studies teacher, was an exception. Having been at Rogers ever since the school opened, he moved to the southwest after teaching in Virginia for three years. His move to the southwest was prompted largely by a chronic case of asthma. On several occasions, Mr. Carson raised the issue of corporal punishment in faculty meetings; he distributed articles to other teachers from professional journals about the effects of corporal punishment; and he had several meetings with the principal to discuss the topic privately. Although he felt very strongly about the principal's methods, Aaron Carson did not take his protestations to the public; that is, until the incident with Jimmy Longbow.

Every student at Rogers Middle School knew Jimmy Longbow. He was a gifted athlete and prone to get into trouble. Jimmy lived with his mother and two sisters. His father passed away several years ago, when he was only thirty-four years old. Jimmy was a student in Aaron Carson's social studies class. It was one of the few classes in which he was making a better than average grade. Aaron saw something in Jimmy that he liked. Maybe he saw a little of himself—a rebellious child, growing up in poverty, without a father, and with a big chip on his shoulder. Aaron remembers all too well his own childhood in Brooklyn, New York. Life was tough and you had to grow up in a hurry.

One of Jimmy's other teachers was Ned Draycroft. Jimmy hated Mr. Draycroft's English class. Poetry, short stories, and diagraming sentences were all things Jimmy did not like to do. One day Jimmy was being verbally disciplined by Mr. Draycroft for not doing his homework. It was a day that the teacher was in an especially bad mood, and Mr. Draycroft was known as a very moody person. The student received a real tongue lashing before the entire class. When Mr. Draycroft finally ended his three-minute diatribe, Jimmy looked him squarely in the eye and said, "This stuff is all crap. Why don't you teach us something that is important?"

The students could see the veins pop out in Mr. Draycroft's neck. He stood in front of the rebellious student and shook his finger. "You, young man, are going to the office. I have had it with you. Maybe a dozen good whacks from the board of education will teach you not to be so impudent."

Mr. Draycroft took Jimmy to the office and told the principal what had happened. Jimmy and Mr. Sanchez were not strangers. There was word among the students that no one had more contact with the board of education than Jimmy.

"Jimmy," Mr. Sanchez began, "when are you going to learn? You mess up, you're going to get it. You can't just shoot your mouth off anytime you feel like it.

It's about time you grew up. But as we see by this incident, you're not there yet. So, you have to be treated like a second grader."

The principal then issued his customary order in these situations, directing the student to empty his back pockets, to bend over, and to hold his ankles. But this time, Jimmy refused to comply.

"You're not going to hit me with that paddle again," he told the principal. "You can take your school and shove it."

With that, Jimmy ran from the office and the school building. Before anyone could catch him, he was gone. The principal called Jimmy's mother who was a waitress in a local diner. She left work immediately to see if she could find her son, but the effort proved fruitless. Jimmy did not come home that night, nor the next, nor the next.

Various accounts of the incident spread quickly through the school. Aaron Carson found out about it in the teachers' lounge. He immediately called Jimmy's mother and asked if he could stop by the house to talk to her. The two had spoken with each other on several occasions about Jimmy's progress at school, so they were not total strangers. Mrs. Longbow trusted Mr. Carson and she shared with him the details of the incident as they were relayed to her by the principal. Aaron assured her that he would do what he could to find Jimmy and indicated he planned to talk to the principal as well.

When Aaron Carson and Pete Sanchez met the next day in the principal's office, the exchange of words was anything but pleasant. Aaron accused the principal of being a bully and a terrible administrator. The principal countered by describing the teacher as a "bleeding heart." It was obvious that the two had very different perceptions about how to handle problem children. Thus it was no surprise that the two ended the meeting the same way they started it, shouting unpleasant remarks to each other.

Aaron decided to take the matter to Mr. Sanchez's supervisor, Dr. Penelope Mackee. He quickly discovered that she was not about to take any action against the principal. She dismissed the matter as rather routine, suggesting that the dispute between the principal and teacher ought to be settled at the school level. Aaron's perception of his meeting with Dr. Mackee was that she was too insecure to take action against a principal who had become somewhat of a legend and hero in the city. The encounter with her only made Aaron angrier and more determined to see that something was done about this situation. He decided to state his case to the media. He wrote the following letter to the editor of the major newspaper in the city:

The public needs to know the story of Jimmy Longbow, a young Indian student at Rogers Middle School who is now a runaway. Jimmy is no angel; but, neither is he some type of second-class citizen who should be whipped every time he does something improper. Corporal punishment is a practice that has been discontinued in most U.S. public schools. But it is alive and well at Rogers Middle School. Jimmy Longbow is now somewhere on the streets because his teachers and his principal thought that brutality was more effective than counseling and constructive behavior modification. Parents of Rogers Middle School students and citizens of this community, wake up! Wake up before it is too late. Let your school board members know what you think about corporal punishment. Let's put a stop to this. Hopefully, Jimmy Longbow will come home, re-enter school, and prove that he can be successful. Let's do something before there are more tragic stories.

Sincerely,

Aaron Carson
Social Studies Teacher
Rogers Middle School

The letter spawned over 300 calls from angry citizens to the school board who supported Mr. Carson's position. The newspaper seized the story and did a three-part report on what had occurred with Jimmy Longbow. The stories were great copy, and the "Jimmy Longbow Incident" became a focused issue throughout the city. Conversely, a large number of parents, especially Rogers Middle School parents, came to the defense of Mr. Sanchez. They wrote their own letters to the newspaper detailing the great work that the principal had done for the school and pledging their support for his leadership. Some supporters of the principal attacked Aaron Carson, labeling him a troublemaker who was simply jealous of Mr. Sanchez's success.

School board members were increasingly disturbed by all the telephone calls and negative publicity. They demanded that the issue be discussed at the next school board meeting. When the newspaper reported that the board had decided to examine the issue publicly, the parent committees at Rogers Middle School started passing the following petition:

We the undersigned fully support the leadership of Mr. Pete Sanchez. He has made Rogers Middle School the most successful school in the district. We believe it is unfair to judge him on the basis of one incident. It is unfair for him to be blamed for what happened to Jimmy Longbow. We urge you, our representatives on the school board, to proclaim your support for a great principal. Further, we believe that in the best interests of Rogers, Mr. Carson should be transferred to another school.

In one week, nearly 70 percent of the Rogers's parents signed the petition. They were mailed three days before the board meeting to each board member and to the superintendent, Dr. Fred Lopson.

The meeting drew more than 400 supporters of Mr. Sanchez. Dr. Lopson began his review of the situation by reminding the board members that existing policy did not prohibit corporal punishment. He also pointed out the distinguished record of the school and the massive parental support enjoyed by its principal. The superintendent also expressed his personal sadness that Jimmy Longbow had run away from home.

George Manulita, a board member and himself a native American, asked to be recognized after the superintendent concluded his remarks.

"I think we are all aware of Mr. Sanchez's successes," he said. "In my opinion, that is not the real issue here. I want to know what we are going to do about allowing corporal punishment in our schools. It's unfortunate that this incident with the student at Rogers Middle School occurred. Hopefully, he will be found and he will return to school. But our concern as board members should now focus on the future. I want to know, Dr. Lopson, what you recommend with regard to policies governing corporal punishment. Do you think we should continue to permit such activity? Should we pass a new policy to prohibit it?"

Mr. Manulita's questions were answered with shouts of "no" from most in the audience.

Darren Marshall, another board member, was next to speak.

"I don't disagree that we ought to think about policies when necessary. But let's keep in mind that we're talking about one of our best schools. Do we want to present yet another barrier to our administrators, especially when this administrator, Mr. Sanchez, is getting the job done? I'm more concerned with what we do about a teacher who writes derogatory letters to the newspaper about his principal. What are we going to do about this, Mr. Superintendent?"

This time the crowd applauded and started to chant, "Mr. Sanchez, Mr. Sanchez."

THE CHALLENGE: Place yourself in the superintendent's position. How would you respond to the two board members?

KEY ISSUES/QUESTIONS:

1. Do you think the parents are correct in linking the discipline practices of the principal with the successes of the school?
2. What are your impressions of Mr. Sanchez? Would you like to be a teacher in his building?
3. Do you see any relationship between the principal's personal life and his philosophy toward discipline?
4. What are your impressions of the teacher who wrote the letter to the newspaper? Could he have addressed the problem in some other way?
5. What are your impressions of the assistant superintendent, Dr. Mackee? Did she adequately address her responsibilities in this incident?
6. What does the literature say about the effectiveness of corporal punishment?
7. How does corporal punishment fit with the goals of middle grades education?
8. If the superintendent decides to examine policy in the area of corporal punishment, how might he go about it?
9. What are the advantages and disadvantages of recommending a transfer for Aaron Carson?
10. In this case, committees are used by the principal to involve parents in the educational process. Under such circumstances, shouldn't the recommendations of these parents play a pivotal role in determining whether the principal is allowed to administer corporal punishment?

11. Consider the support for the principal in the context of the social and economic dimensions of the neighborhoods served by Rogers Middle School.

SUGGESTED READINGS:

Andrews, R., & Soder, R. (1987). Principal leadership and student achievement. *Educational Leadership, 44*(6), 9–11.

Auer, M., & Nisenholz, B. (1987). Humanistic processes and bureaucratic structures—Are they compatible? *NASSP Bulletin, 71*(495), 95–101.

Carey, M. (1986). School discipline: Better to be loved or feared? *Momentum, 17*(2), 20–21.

Eberts, R., & Stone, J. (1988). Student achievement in public schools: Do principals make a difference? *Economics of Education Review, 7*(3), 291–299.

Erickson, H. (1988). The boy who couldn't be disciplined. *Principal, 67*(5), 36–37.

deJung, J., & Duckworth, K. (1985). *An examination of student discipline policy in three middle schools: Final report.* ERIC, Document Number ED256018.

Glassman, N. (1986). Student achievement and the school principal. *Education Evaluation and Policy Analysis, 7*(2), 283–296.

Helms, M. (1985). *Bureaucracy and social interaction: A study in the perceived interaction between a superintendent and campus principals.* Unpublished Ph.D. thesis, University of North Texas.

Kritsonis, W., & Adams, S. (1985/86). School discipline: Could I be part of the problem? *National Forum of Educational Administration and Supervision, 2*(2), 68–72.

Lowe, R., & Gervais, R. (1984). Tackling a problem school. *Principal, 63*(5), 8–12.

Maurer, A. (1981). *Paddles away: A psychological study of physical punishment in schools.* Palo Alto, CA: R & E Research Associates.

McDaniel, T. (1986). School discipline in perspective. *Clearing House, 59*(8), 369–370.

Nolte, M. (1985). Before you take a paddling in court, read this corporal punishment advice. *American School Board Journal, 173*(7), 27, 35.

Paquet, R. (1982). *Judicial rulings, state statutes, and state administrative regulations dealing with the use of corporal punishment in public schools.* Palo Alto, CA: R & E Research Associates.

Reavis, C. (1986). How a lighthouse principal revitalized his school. *NASSP Bulletin, 70*(492), 44–49.

Rose, T. (1984). Current uses of corporal punishment in American public schools. *Journal of Educational Psychology, 76*(3), 427–441.

Slavin, R., & Madden, N. (1989). What works for students at-risk: A research synthesis. *Educational Leadership, 46*(5), 4–13.

Webster, L., et al. (1988). Attitudes of rural administrators toward corporal punishment. *Journal of Rural and Small Schools, 3*(1), 19–22.

Zirkel, P., & Gluckman, I. (1988). A legal brief: Constitutionalizing corporal punishment. *NASSP Bulletin, 72*(506), 105–109.

CASE 13

The Stepping Stone

Entering the 20th Century

THE COMMUNITY

Hallville is located in northern Iowa. It is a friendly town of about 2,500 residents, many of whom have never lived anywhere else. Besides the bank, the Sears outlet store, Dotty's restaurant, an IGA grocery store, two taverns, and Klink's Farm Implement, there is not much else downtown. Being twenty-seven miles from the county seat, a community of 65,000, Hallville's residents have become accustomed to traveling elsewhere to meet their special needs.

Most everyone in Hallville knows everyone else. The town picnics, one in early June and one in late August, are the social highlights of the year. Loretta Helmich is mayor, but it is only a part-time job that she does when she is not working at the bank. The police department consists of one full-time and two part-time officers. There is very little crime in Hallville.

Most Hallville residents are connected in some way with the corn processing plant located on the edge of town. It is not a very big operation, but it is highly successful. The town is surrounded by farms, many of them large operations of 400 or more acres.

THE SCHOOLS

Hallville Community School District includes two attendance centers: Hallville Junior/Senior High School and Hallville Elementary School. The basic information for each school is as follows:

Hallville Junior–Senior High School
- grade levels: 7–12
- enrollment: 440
- principal: Oscar McCammick
- assistant principal: Judy Buschak
- number of teachers: 26
- number of counselors: 1
- number of secretaries: 2
- custodians: 3
- other personnel (cooks, aides, etc.): 9

Hallville Elementary School
- grade levels: K–6
- enrollment: 407
- principal: Denise Fischer
- number of teachers: 18
- number of counselors: 1
- number of secretaries: 2
- custodians: 2
- other personnel (cooks, aides, etc.): 13

The junior/senior high school is a relatively new structure erected six years ago. The elementary school is a much older facility, built circa 1955. The two schools are located on different sites. The elementary school is in the town, the junior/senior high school is located just outside of town on the state highway.

Last year, Wilbur Stineman, the superintendent, was killed in an automobile accident on his way home from a meeting in Des Moines. His entire career was spent in the Hallville school district. He was a teacher, coach, counselor, and eventually principal at the high school before being named superintendent. His death stunned the community. He was respected and well-liked.

Almost everyone took for granted that Oscar McCammick, the principal at the junior/senior high school would take over as superintendent. But the veteran administrator surprised the five-member school board when he announced he was not interested in the job. He said he liked what he was doing and especially enjoyed working with the students. For the first time in more than fifty years, Hallville had to hire a superintendent from outside of the school district.

The unanimous choice of the school board for superintendent was Rob Zelker. Rob was only thirty-one years old, but he was a mature person who related well to the school board members. For the past three years, he had been a principal in an elementary school in one of the larger cities in Iowa. Rob recently completed his specialist's degree at a state university and obtained his certification as a superintendent. The school board was impressed by the fact that Rob grew up in a community in western Iowa very similar to Hallville. He was a "farm boy" who understood the people; thus although he was not from Hallville, his personal background was congruent with the environment.

The selection procedure for the superintendent included participation by the school district staff and parents. When Rob was invited to visit Hallville by the school board, three separate interview sessions were arranged: one with the board, one with a committee representing the employees of the school district, and one with a parent committee. He was the choice of all three groups. His appointment was especially supported by the two principals in the school district who also had an opportunity to meet the finalists for the position.

THE NEW SUPERINTENDENT

Rob's wife, Alice, a nurse, was able to get a part-time position working for a local physician in Hallville. Their daughter, Amy, is in first grade. Rob and Alice did not intend to stay in Hallville more than three years, so they decided to rent.

Rob Zelker viewed the job at Hallville as a stepping stone for his career in educational administration. He applied and was accepted for a doctoral program at a university some forty-five miles from his residence. His plan was to spend three years in this school district and to take some occasional courses toward his final degree. Then he planned to leave Hallville.

Prior to accepting the job at Hallville, Rob had a lengthy conversation with Dr. Nolan Smythe, the superintendent in the district where he worked as an elementary principal. During Rob's tenure as a building administrator, he developed a close relationship with his superintendent. This occurred even though principals did not report directly to the superintendent in this large district. But Rob and Dr. Smythe were both active in the same church, and it was no secret that the superintendent liked the young principal. In fact, it was Dr. Smythe who advised Rob to pursue the job in Hallville and to enroll in a doctoral program.

Rob idolized Superintendent Smythe. He meticulously observed this leader's behavior in different situations. Bob watched the way he handled meetings with staff and the school board; he studied the superintendent's demeanor around the central office; and, he especially took notice of Dr. Smythe's approach to dealing with conflict. Being in a city of about 100,000 residents, the superintendent had myriad opportunities for visibility—and Dr. Smythe took advantage of most. Among other things, he was on the board of directors of a bank, secretary of the Chamber of Commerce, and the president of the city's country club.

Nolan Smythe dressed and acted like a corporate executive. He often commented to Rob that personal appearance was extremely important if you wanted those around you to respect you as a leader. Before Rob left for the challenge of his first superintendency, he spent several evenings talking to Dr. Smythe, trying to squeeze every possible ounce of advice out of his mentor.

THE FIRST YEAR IN HALLVILLE

The central administrative offices for the Hallville Community School District are located in a wing of the junior/senior high school. There are only three persons who are officially part of the central office staff: a secretary, a bookkeeper, and the superintendent. The secretary, Bonnie Stutz, is the sister of one of the school board members. The bookkeeper, Norine Dawson, is a widow. Both employees have lived in Hallville their entire lives and both have been with the school system in excess of twenty years.

On the very first day as superintendent in Hallville, Rob ordered some new furniture for his office. The other thing he did was visit his two principals, Oscar McCammick and Judy Fischer. That evening at dinner, Rob shared some perceptions regarding his new position with his wife.

"You know, Alice, this is a sleepy little town and I expected things to be a bit informal. But you wouldn't believe just how informal they really are. When I walked across the building to see the principal, Oscar McCammick was sitting in his office talking with several teachers. When he saw me, he yelled for me to come on in. The secretary was no where to be found. Oscar was sitting with feet up on desk and he wasn't even wearing a tie."

"Well," his wife answered, "maybe he just doesn't get dressed up during the summer. It is July you know. I bet when school starts, he'll look like any other principal."

Rob shrugged his shoulders as it to indicate that his wife may be right. Then he told his wife about the visit to elementary school.

"When I got to the elementary school, there's the secretary sitting there listening to the radio. She didn't know who I was. I asked to see Mrs. Fischer and she told me she'd be back in an hour or so. She said the principal had an appointment to get her hair done. Can you believe this?"

During the next few months Rob realized that what he witnessed the first day was not atypical. Even school board meetings were extremely informal with every one using first names and persons in the audience allowed to speak just about any time they asked to be recognized. What particularly irked the superintendent was that all the employees, even custodians, called him by his first name. Rob became convinced that his youth had a great deal to do with the way people were treating him. But he was also convinced that the casual climate in the school system generated managerial inefficiency. In late October, he decided it was time to change a few things.

Rob's first step to instituting change was to set meetings with the two central office employees and with the two principals. He shared his observations after being superintendent for just three months and indicated that he found it a bit embarrassing that the school administration functioned so informally. He emphatically stated that he wanted the following directives carried out:

1. The principals and two employees of the central office were to set an example by addressing him as Mr. Zelker, especially in the presence of others.
2. The secretary was never to call him Rob when talking to a third party on the telephone.

3. Visitors should never be allowed to enter the office of administrators without first making a request with a secretary.

4. In the future, communications among the central office employees and the school administrators should be conducted via written memoranda.

Although all four employees were unhappy with these directives, none was willing to take exception with the orders. Bonnie Stutz did tell her brother, a school board member, that she thought the whole thing was stupid.

After setting new directions for his key employees, Rob turned his attention to the school board. He developed a lengthly memorandum recommending changes in the way school board meetings would be conducted. Included were suggestions that the board take formal votes on motions, that the men wear coats and ties to board meetings, and that the board set rules regarding public participation in the meetings. The memorandum prompted a visit from the board president.

Dale Klink owns the farm implement store in Hallville and he has been president of the school board for three years. Dale does not like to interfere in the day-to-day operations of the school district and he only goes over to see the superintendent when it's absolutely necessary. The superintendent's memorandum, he decided, created one of those occasions.

The two men met on a dreary mid-November day in the administrative offices. After getting a cup of coffee and saying hello to the two women, the board president went in the superintendent's office and shut the door.

"Rob, what the hell possessed you to send this memo to the board? Don't you think that it would have been better to call me and tell me you were concerned about some things before writing to the entire board? You know, this is a little embarrassing for me."

The abrupt statements of the board president immediately put the superintendent on the defensive. Rob figured that some board members would object to his recommendations, but he never thought the reaction would be so sudden and swift. He collected his thoughts before responding.

"Dale, I certainly did not want to embarrass anyone. I'm just trying to make this a better school district. I thought that is why you hired me. If I was out of line sending the memorandum, I'm sorry. But I must honestly tell you, I don't think that I was."

"Rob, you've been here three months now. In that short time, you've managed to get the principals all riled; and the gals here in the office aren't too happy about your demands either," the board president said.

"This is a good school district," answered the superintendent, "but it could be a lot better. There is a tremendous amount of inefficiency around here. It's not the informality, per se, that bothers me. It's the attitudes and behavior that are associated with the informality. Employees think they can leave work whenever they feel like it to go to the bank, to buy groceries, or get their hair done. And when the administrators and central office staff are doing these things, how can we expect other employees to be any different. I believe that good examples have to start at the very top. That's why I suggested we make our board meetings more dignified."

The board president took a drink of his coffee and stood up. He looked at the young superintendent and said,

"Rob, I've got to get back to my store. But let me tell you before I leave that you've got a lot to learn. This is a nice community. We've never had trouble with superintendents and we don't want to start now. But let me tell you, you're not going to come in here and change everything in a few months. We're not going to change the board meetings. You're the one who needs to consider changing. The best thing you can do is forget you ever wrote this memorandum to the board. Think it over, Rob. You have a good job and I hope you don't decide to throw it all away."

That said, Dale Klink walked out of the office. Rob's heart was beating and he had little beads of perspiration on the back of his neck. He knew he was in trouble and he was not sure what he should do. He tried to reach his trusted advisor, Dr. Nolan Smythe, but he was on a trip to the Soviet Union with a group of educators.

THE CHALLENGE: Assume the role of the young superintendent in this case. What would you do?

KEY ISSUES/QUESTIONS

1. To what extent do you think that Rob's attitude about going to Hallville affects his behavior in this case?
2. Was the board correct in assuming that, because Rob grew up in a small town similar to Hallville, he would be able to affectively work there?
3. To what extent is the behavior of the principals described in this study typical or atypical for small town/rural school districts?
4. Is it common for young administrators to try to emulate the behavior of someone they admire?
5. Discuss the various types of power. What type of power did Dr. Smythe have over Rob?
6. What are the advantages and disadvantages of the following:
   a. the superintendent resigning immediately
   b. the superintendent apologizing to the board and agreeing that he will work to change his behavior and attitudes?
7. Is the superintendent's assessment that informality breeds inefficiency accurate? Why or why not?
8. Do you think the school board knows that Rob is only planning to stay in Hallville for three years? What leads you to your conclusion?
9. What alternatives could Rob have pursued to implement change in the school district?
10. Did Rob do the right thing by trying to emulate the successful practices of an outstanding superintendent?

SUGGESTED READINGS:

Alvey, D., & Underwood, K. (1985). When boards and superintendents clash, it's over the balance of school power. *American School Board Journal, 172*(10), 21–25.

Black, J., & English, F. (1986). *What they don't tell you in schools of education about school administration,* pp. 293–307, Lancaster, PA: Technomic.

Boynton, M. (1985). *Principal P. R. techniques for small schools.* ERIC, Document Number ED270281.

Campion, M., & Lord, R. (1982). A control systems conceptualization of the goal-setting and changing process. *Organizational Behavior and Human Performance, 30,* 265–287.

Clark, D., & Astuto, T. (1988). Paradoxical choice options in organizations. In D. Griffiths, R. Stout, & P. Forsyth (Eds.), *Leaders for America's schools,* pp. 112–130. Berkeley, CA: McCutchan.

Guthrie, J., & Reed, R. (1986). *Educational administration and policy,* pp. 166–175. Englewood Cliffs, NJ: Prentice-Hall.

Fuqua, A. (1983). *Professional attractiveness, inside sponsorship, and perceived paternalism as predictors of upward mobility of public school superintendents.* Unpublished Ph.D. thesis, Virginia Polytechnic Institute and State University.

Immegart, G. (1988). Leadership and leader behavior. In N. Boyan (Ed.), *Handbook of research on educational administration,* pp. 259–277. White Plains, NY: Longman.

Jacobson, S. (1988). Effective superintendents of small, rural districts. *Journal of Rural and Small Schools, 2*(2), 17–21.

Oberg, T. (1986). The ecstasy and the agony: Administrative success on one level does not guarantee success on another. *Journal of Educational Public Relations, 9*(2), 28–31.

Schaal, B. (1987). *Perceived conflict among Wisconsin superintendents and its relationship to selected factors.* Unpublished Ph.D. thesis, University of Nebraska, Lincoln.

Sergiovanni, T., Burlingame, M., Coombs, F., & Thurston, P. (1987). *Educational governance and administration* (2nd ed.), pp. 206–219, 384–416. Englewood Cliffs, NJ: Prentice-Hall.

St. John, J. (1985). *Superintendents' leadership style and communication satisfaction.* Unpublished Ed.D. thesis, Northern Illinois University.

Toy, S. (1985). Use this ten point plan to bolster community rapport. *Executive Educator, 7*(6), 23–25.

Yukl, G. (1989). *Leadership in organizations* (2nd ed.), chap. 8. Englewood Cliffs, NJ: Prentice-Hall.

CASE 14

Success Is Spelled "PR, PR, PR"

One of Peter Marini's earliest memories of Wellington was of a demolition project in the downtown area. Two large stores that were more than 100 years old were flattened by a bulldozer as he drove his new Buick down Main Street. The scene did little to lift the spirits of this successful administrator who had accepted the invitation of the local school board to interview for the superintendency of the city's school district with mixed feelings. All during the long drive from eastern Pennsylvania, Peter kept mentally asking himself why he was making the trip. He was currently superintendent of an outstanding district, and he really did not need a new job. But several placement consultants convinced him to take a look at the job in Wellington.

Now several years later, he was driving down Main Street and he saw that construction was taking place on the vacant lots. A new office building was being erected on the very spot where the old stores had been razed a couple of years ago. But as he drove slowly down the street, Peter Marini no longer thought about the future of Wellington. His mind now focused on a very different problem.

Wellington is one of the larger cities in this New England state. It is an industrial community that fell on hard times during the 1970s and 1980s. Unlike many other cities suffering the same conditions, Wellington was able to turn things around. The upward trend in economics and politics started about the time that Dan Ferriter was elected mayor. An energetic attorney who served two terms in the state legislature, Mayor Ferriter set out to bring new business to the city.

The same year that there was a change in the mayor's office, the superintendent of the Wellington City Schools resigned to accept a position in another state. Mayor Ferriter believed that the school district had many strengths that could prove vital to his efforts to breathe new life into the city. He successfully convinced the school board to retain the services of Dr. Alex Porter, a professor at the state university, to assist in securing a dynamic chief executive for the school district. Dr. Porter was an experienced "head hunter" who had worked with many school boards in the east. Upon being retained by the Wellington board, the professor successfully convinced the board members that: (1) they would have to pursue good candidates rather than sitting back and hoping good candidates would come to them, and (2) they would have to pay a top salary to get an outstanding superintendent. The board agreed to the recommendations. Furthermore, they identified the following qualifications for their new superintendent:

1. The person must have a minimum of three years of experience as a superintendent, preferably in a larger city district.
2. The person must possess outstanding skills in public relations.
3. The person must be able to deal with all elements of the community and be willing to actively participate in a variety of community functions.
4. The person must relate well to staff and possess exceptional communication skills.
5. The person must know how to effectively delegate authority.

Of all of the stated qualifications, it was the public relations aspect that loomed as the greatest priority in the minds of the school board and Mayor Ferriter. As a state legislator, Dan Ferriter observed how school districts won recognition more on what people believed they did than on what they had actually done. Thus, he urged the board to employ someone who could create the proper image of the school district—an image that would assist the city in convincing businesses and residents that Wellington was a great place to work and live.

The assistance of Dr. Porter proved fruitful and the school board was able to hire Dr. Peter Marini. He had all the right qualifications. He was the superintendent of a large suburban district in eastern Pennsylvania; he is a dynamic and charismatic leader; his forte is public relations; and he has a doctorate from an Ivy League university. Luring him to Wellington was not easy, but the salary of $125,000 helped.

The Wellington City School District consists of three high schools, seven middle schools, and twenty-two elementary schools. Overall, there are about 22,000 students enrolled in the district. The central office has a professional staff of twenty-four.

After accepting the job in Wellington, Dr. Marini reorganized some of the central office positions. Most notably, he elevated one of the three associate superintendents to the position of deputy superintendent. He selected Dr. Teresa Howard for the newly created post. She was a veteran administrator, well-liked in the district. At age fifty-one, she had spent over twenty years in the school system as a teacher and administrator. In structuring the deputy's role, Peter Marini made an attempt to hide his expectations that the person holding this position would be responsible for managing the day-to-day operations of the school district.

As might be expected, the superintendent and the mayor became friends and associates in the effort to promote Wellington. Both were adept at building positive images. From the very first few weeks in Wellington to the present, Superintendent Marini spent very little time in his office or in the schools. Rather, he did as the school board expected. He met with community groups, visited with executives of companies considering locating in Wellington, and spent a great deal of time working with the mayor and his staff.

The school district did quite well even though the superintendent devoted little time tending to customary duties of the executive leader of a school system. Numerous academic awards and honors coupled with successes in athletics made the work of the superintendent and mayor even easier. Every time the school district won an award, Superintendent Marini always made time to be at the award ceremony and made sure there were plenty of photographers.

Somewhere during the winter of his second year in Wellington, Peter recognized a distinctive change in his deputy superintendent. She had become impatient and started complaining about all the work she had to do. Peter was an experienced leader and he knew something was wrong. He scheduled a three-hour luncheon with his deputy in hopes of determining the nature of the problem.

The two met in the superintendent's office and had lunch brought in. Peter started out by telling Dr. Howard that he very much appreciated the outstanding work she was doing. He reminded her that he recommended a 10 percent salary increase for her last year. But then he turned to his concern.

"Theresa, you don't seem yourself these days. Is anything wrong?"

"Would it matter if there was something wrong?" she responded.

"Our working relationship," Peter said, "is extremely important if we are to keep this school district and city moving forward. Yes, I do care how you feel and I do want to know if something is wrong."

The deputy sat there for a moment and then looked up at Peter and said, "I really don't know where to begin. But here goes. The staff here in the central office are concerned—no, let me rephrase that. I am concerned about the fact that you know very little about what is going on in this school district. You go to school board meetings and you have to be briefed on everything so you can discuss the items with the board. I just don't think that is a good situation."

Peter asked, "Is this a concern for most of the central office staff?"

"Yes."

"What else are they, or you, concerned about?" he asked.

"I don't want to speak for the staff; but I guess I might as well lay the cards on the table as far as I'm concerned," she said. "I feel I'm running the district and you are getting all the credit. Last week at the annual Chamber of Commerce meeting, Mayor Ferriter gave you a special plaque recognizing your leadership in the school district and the community. You never once acknowledged how much help you get from your staff. Then there's the matter of salary. You are making over $125,000, not to mention fringe benefits. I'm making $40,000 less and running the school district. Do you think that is fair?"

"Theresa, the board brought me to this community to do certain things. I believe I am doing those things and doing them well. You knew when I named you deputy that you would be in charge of the day-to-day management of the district. I don't think anyone has tried to take advantage of you."

"I work darn hard, Peter, and you know it. I get here early and leave late every day. Who knows what you're doing? Some of the secretaries in the central office don't even know who you are. You rarely visit any of the schools except to collect awards and make speeches at events that have a public relations benefit."

At that point the deputy paused, and Peter could see she was really upset. He remained quiet while she regained her composure.

"Look, Peter, let me be as blunt as I can. If you're not willing to pay me more money, and I don't just mean a couple of thousand dollars, and if you're not willing to see that my accomplishments receive due consideration, I don't think I want to go on in this job. Now you think that over and let me know what you decide."

At that point, Theresa got up and left the office before Peter could respond.

The meeting with his deputy superintendent affected Peter. He realized that he had not gotten to know Theresa. He tried to imagine being in her position. Would he react in the same way? He wondered if he should replace her in the deputy's position. He wondered if he was as self-centered as Theresa suggested. He even wondered if he should leave Wellington.

Driving down Main Street seemed to provide inspiration for Peter whenever he had to make a difficult decision. Given the problem with Dr. Theresa Howard, he decided to make a couple of slow trips down the street. This time, however, the answer did not come easily.

THE CHALLENGE: Place yourself in Dr. Marini's position. What would you do with regard to the deputy superintendent?

KEY ISSUES/QUESTIONS:

1. Do you believe that Dr. Howard is being fair with the superintendent?
2. Is it common for administrative staff members to believe that their work is not properly recognized or compensated?
3. Is Dr. Marini, in your opinion, doing a good job as superintendent? Why or why not?
4. What are the advantages and disadvantages of Dr. Marini deciding to reassign his deputy superintendent?
5. Given the information in this case, do you believe that Dr. Marini is in a position to meet the demands of his deputy?
6. What are the advantages and disadvantages of the superintendent deciding to spend more time working directly with the day-to-day operations of the school district?
7. In school districts of twenty to thirty thousand students, is it common for the superintendent to spend time in the school buildings? What basis do you have for your response?

8. What information is not presented in this case that you think would be important in formulating a response?
9. What could Dr. Marini have done to avoid this confrontation with his deputy?
10. What could Dr. Howard have done to avoid the confrontation?

SUGGESTED READINGS:

Bagin, R. (1984). *Evaluating your school PR investment.* ERIC, Document Number ED264650.

Black, J., & English, F. (1986). *What they don't tell you in schools of education about school administration,* chap. 12. Lancaster, PA: Technomic.

Boyd, W. (Ed.). (1979). *Education and urban society, 11,* 275–431 (special theme issue: Declining school enrollments: Politics and management).

Chand, K. (1984). *Superintendent-community relationships in the United States and Alaska.* ERIC, Document Number ED249616.

Danzberger, J., & Usdan, M. (1984). Building partnerships: The Atlanta experience. *Phi Delta Kappan, 65*(6), 393–396.

Foster, W. (1986). *Paradigms and promises,* chap. 8. Buffalo, NY: Prometheus Books.

Goldhammer, K. (1983). Evolution in the profession. *Educational Administration Quarterly, 19*(3), 249–272.

Hess, F. (1983). Evolution in practice. *Educational Administration Quarterly, 19*(3), 223–248.

Hoy, W., & Miskel, C. (1987). *Educational administration: Theory, research, practice* (3rd ed.), pp. 302–309, New York: Random House.

Lindsay, C. (1986). Try these tonics to pep up schools. *Executive Educator, 8*(4), 28, 38.

Love, R. (1982). *Mayors and superintendents: What techniques might be used to improve partnerships.* ERIC, Document Number ED226440.

McLaughlin, M. (1987). Forge alliances with key groups. *Executive Educator, 9*(11), 21, 30.

Newell, C. (1978). *Human behavior in educational administration,* chap. 10. Englewood Cliffs, NJ: Prentice-Hall.

Pajak, E. (1989). *The central office supervisor of curriculum and instruction,* chap. 4. Boston: Allyn & Bacon.

Sergiovanni, T., Burlingame, M., Coombs, F., & Thurston, P. (1987). *Educational governance and administration* (2nd ed.). chap. 7. Englewood Cliffs, NJ: Prentice-Hall.

Shakeshaft, C. (1989). *Women in educational administration* (updated ed.), chap. 6. Newbury Park, CA: Sage Publications.

Stout, S., et al. (1987). Career transitions of supervisors and subordinates. *Journal of Vocational Behavior, 30*(2), 124–137.

Worner, R. (1989). Thirteen ways to help your inherited staff keep you afloat. *Executive Educator, 11*(5), 19–21.

Yukl, G. (1989). *Leadership in organizations* (2nd ed.), pp. 153–157. Englewood Cliffs, NJ: Prentice-Hall.

CASE 15

Sorcerer Will Help You Spell It

"I really like this program. It would fit in so nicely with our initiatives."

The judgment came from Sandy Oberfeld, a second-grade teacher. She was addressing about twenty of her colleagues in a meeting at Samuels Elementary School. The teachers were evaluating materials that they might infuse into their programs for gifted and talented elementary students.

"I agree," said Beatrice Sachs. "My children like something different. They have so many toys and gadgets at home it's hard to motivate them. I think *Sorcerer* is a novel way to get these children to work independently on their spelling."

The elementary school gifted and talented program in Maple Creek School District, an affluent-midwestern suburb, is clustered in three of the ten elementary schools in the system. The twenty-one teachers who work in the program meet once every two months to discuss materials, share ideas, and the like. At this meeting, the teachers were discussing *Sorcerer*—an instructional game designed to help elementary age children develop spelling skills. Sandy Oberfeld is the coordinator of the group and it was she who introduced the *Sorcerer* program to the other teachers. She saw the materials at a conference and asked the publisher to send her a review copy. After Sandy gave a brief demonstration on how to use the program, her peer teachers requested that sixty-three copies of the materials be purchased (three for each teacher).

The requisition for the purchase of *Sorcerer* was transmitted through Sandy to the assistant superintendent for instruction, Dr. Wilbur Youngman. He manages a special budget established to purchase materials for the gifted and talented program.

On receiving the copies of the *Sorcerer* program, every one of the twenty-one teachers used the materials. Children were allowed to check the programs out to do independent work either at school or home. The game essentially entails a system of rewards and punishments based on the student's success mastering spelling words. The teachers believe that the children really enjoy working with the game because many request to use it.

Within one month after the *Sorcerer* program was introduced in the school system, the first complaint was received. Miss Nancy Tannin, principal at Lakeside Elementary School, received a telephone call from Mrs. Baker, a parent. The call caught the principal off guard.

"Miss Tannin, this is Mrs. Baker, Sally's mother. How are you today?"

"Just fine," answered the principal. She vaguely remembered having met Mrs. Baker at an open house earlier in the school year.

"What can I do for you, Mrs. Baker?"

"Well, I'm calling about a set of materials my daughter brought home. She is in the gifted and talented program, and she regularly brings home books and other materials that are given to her by the teachers. I noticed the other day that she was working with some type of game. It's called *Sorcerer*. You're familiar with it aren't you?"

The principal responded that she was not. But then Miss Tannin went on to tell the mother, "Our teachers use a variety of supplemental materials in the gifted and talented program. I suppose this game you're talking about is something that falls into that category. Is there a particular problem with this game?"

"You bet there is. It's all about witchcraft and magic. It's suppose to be teaching spelling; but if you want my opinion, it's teaching little children some very unhealthy values."

The principal indicated that she would look into the matter and call the mother back. Miss Tannin did not consider the complaint to be a major problem and made no special effort to contact the faculty member immediately. She figured she would inquire about the program the next time she saw the teacher. Two days later, she had the opportunity to make the inquiry and subsequently telephoned Mrs. Baker. She told the mother that neither she nor the teacher saw anything especially evil with the *Sorcerer* program. Mrs. Baker reacted with anger, "Well, this certainly isn't the last you've heard about this. So be prepared."

In that same week, Miss Tannin telephoned the other principals at the cluster schools, Deloris Gragolis and Mitch Sancheck, to see if they have received complaints about *Sorcerer*. They informed her that they had. In each instance, however, the principals said they received positive feedback from the teachers when they mentioned the complaints and raised questions about the program. Given this response from the teachers and the fact that *Sorcerer* is produced and marketed by a reputable software firm, the principals concluded that there must be some basic misunderstanding or misinterpretation on the part of the parents. Thus, no corrective action was taken by the principals.

The issue of *Sorcerer* came up at the next administrative meeting in the school district. The principals wanted Dr. Youngman, the assistant superintendent who authorized the purchase, to be aware of the parental complaints they were receiving. He instructed the principals to monitor the situation and to let him know if the parental concerns persisted. He further advised them to instruct the parents that their children were under no obligation to use the *Sorcerer* programs, because they were simply used for enrichment activities.

True to the warning issued by Mrs. Baker, the parental objections did not subside. They increased in number and became more targeted at the principals. Two weeks after the first call to Miss Tannin at Lakeside Elementary, a letter to the editor appeared in the local newspaper condemning the use of *Sorcerer*.

We are parents of elementary school-age children who participate in the gifted and talented program in the Maple Creek School District. Recently, our children have been exposed to a distasteful and evil set of materials called Sorcerer. These materials are supposed to assist our children with their spelling skills; but in reality, they expose our children to witchcraft and other evil concepts.

The adoption of Sorcerer is yet another example of how our public schools have become a pawn for those who wish to drag our society into the mud. Parents who support our public schools with hard-earned tax dollars should not have to be concerned that positive values taught at home are being eroded by tasteless games in school.

Perhaps the most discouraging element of our complaint is that the school administration appears unwilling to do anything about this situation. Our calls to principals have either been ignored, or they have been answered with suggestions that we don't understand the value of such material. As taxpayers and as parents, we urge others to join our protest. Let's keep our schools free of witchcraft, devil worship, and other evil concepts. Call your school board member now!

(This letter to the editor was signed by forty-six parents.)

Superintendent Philip Montgomery received calls from four of the seven school board members within twenty-four hours of the letter appearing in the newspaper. He gave each board member the same answer, he would look into the situation immediately.

Dr. Montgomery called his assistant, Dr. Youngman, and asked him to set up a meeting with the three principals and Mrs. Oberfeld, the coordinating teacher in the gifted and talent program. The meeting was held in the superintendent's conference room two days later. Dr. Montgomery asked for a full explanation of how the materials were purchased and he asked the teachers to demonstrate how they are used.

After viewing the software the superintendent commented, "This program is similar to a game called Dungeons and something that all the kids were playing a few years ago. That game got some negative publicity. Maybe that's what this is all about."

Mrs. Oberfeld said, "These parents who are complaining belong to a fundamentalist church. They are being told to complain. At least that is what I hear."

Dr. Montgomery asked the principals to comment on the matter. None was especially willing to do so. Miss Tannin decided that some comment was necessary.

"We didn't have anything to do with purchasing these materials. The teachers asked for *Sorcerer* and Dr. Youngman authorized the purchase. Now it seems we are being put on the spot. I don't really think it should be up to us to decide."

Dr. Youngman reacted, "Well, I did approve of the purchase, but I think principals have to maintain some degree of responsibility for what is used in the individual schools. I recommend that each school decide whether to continue using the game."

Mrs. Oberfeld was disturbed by what she was hearing. "Are we going to allow a group of parents, a small group at that, to dictate what we do in our schools. I think that giving in to these individuals will only convince them to seek other restrictions. These are persons who believe in censorship. They want to control what people read and how they think."

One by one the three principals told the superintendent that they really did not want to get mixed up in this matter. They wanted Dr. Youngman and/or the superintendent to decide the future of *Sorcerer*. As Mr. Sancheck put it, "We are here to carry out policy. Whatever you decide, we'll go along."

As the meeting progressed, Dr. Montgomery reached three conclusions: (1) the teachers would probably react negatively if *Sorcerer* were removed from the list of resource materials used in the gifted and talented program, (2) none of the administrators in the meeting was willing to recommend either the removal or continuance of the program, and (3) the parental complaints were not likely to simply disappear. Mostly out of a sense of frustration, he called the meeting to an end. He sat in the conference room long after the others left and pondered what he would tell the school board at their upcoming meeting in three days.

THE CHALLENGE: Place yourself in Dr. Montgomery's position. What would you do about *Sorcerer?*

KEY ISSUES/QUESTIONS:

1. Evaluate the process for purchasing materials for the gifted and talented program in the school district.
2. Whom do you believe should be held accountable for this problem?
3. Is it sufficent to tell the parents, as Dr. Youngman suggested to the principals, that use of the materials is voluntary? Why or why not?
4. Is there anything about the community in which this occurs that has implications for potential solutions?
5. What is your assessment of the position taken by the three elementary principals?
6. What is your assessment of Dr. Youngman's behavior in this case?
7. Relate the problem in this case with the movement toward teacher empowerment.
8. What are the advantages and disadvantages of the superintendent deciding to support Mrs. Oberfeld and keeping the program among the supplemental materials in the gifted and talented curriculum?
9. Identify an alternative method for selecting instructional materials that may have avoided this problem.
10. Do you agree with the assessment of Mrs. Oberfeld that there are fundamentalist-type parents who want to control the entire curriculum of public schools?

SUGGESTED READINGS:

Bailey, G. (1988). Guidelines for improving the textbook/material selection process. *NASSP Bulletin, 72*(515), 87–92.

Bryson, J. (1983). *Conservative pressures on curriculum.* ERIC, Document Number ED232307.

DeRoche, E. (1985). *How administrators solve problems,* chap. 9. Englewood Cliffs, NJ: Prentice-Hall.

Donelson, K. (1987). Censorship: Heading off the attack. *Educational Horizons, 65,* 167–170.

Donelson, K. (1987). Six statements/questions from the censors. *Phi Delta Kappan, 69,* 208–214.

Georgiady, N., & Romano, L. (1987). Censorship—Back to the front burner. *Middle School Journal, 18,* 12–13.

Guthrie, J., & Reed, R. (1986). *Educational administration and policy,* pp. 333–343. Englewood Cliffs, NJ: Prentice-Hall.

McCarthy, M. (1985). Curriculum controversies and the law. *Educational Horizons, 64*(3), 53–55.

McCarthy, M. (1988). Curriculum censorship: Values in conflict. *Educational Horizons, 67*(1–2), 26–34.

Pajak, E. (1989). *The central office supervisor of curriculum and instruction,* chap. 11. Boston: Allyn & Bacon.

Pierard, R. (1983). What's new about the new right. *Contemporary Education, 54*(3), 194–200.

Pierard, R. (1987). The new religious right and censorship. *Contemporary Education, 58*(3), 131–137.

Rowell, C. (1986). Allowing parents to screen textbooks would lead to anarchy in the schools. *Chronicle of Higher Education, 33* (November 26), 34.

Snyder, K., & Anderson, R. (1986). *Managing productive schools: Toward an ecology,* pp. 333–341. Orlando, FL: Academic Press College Division.

Weil, J. (1988). Dealing with censorship: Policy and procedures. *Education Digest, 53*(5), 23–25.

Zirkel, P., & Gluckman, I. (1986). Objections to curricular material on religious grounds. *NASSP Bulletin, 70*(488), 99–100.

CASE 16

Whose Philosophy Will Control Collective Bargaining?

Two years ago Janice Melton achieved her primary professional goal. At age 42, she was named superintendent of the third largest school district in her state. It was quite an accomplishment considering that she was the first female ever to be superintendent of a district of over 5,000 students in this western state and one of only five female superintendents in the entire state.

Janice grew up in an "education" family. Her father was a teacher and middle school principal for forty-one years. Her mother taught kindergarten in the public schools for eleven years and was a professor of early childhood education at a local college for the remainder of her career. Given the influences of her parents, Janice never really thought about entering a profession other than education. After teaching high school English for five years, she returned to graduate school on a full-time basis to complete her doctorate in educational administration. It was during these years of graduate school that Janice met and married Bob.

Bob is a rather successful freelance writer. His work has appeared in a number of leading magazines including *Reader's Digest*. His career produces an ample income, and he could easily support his family without Janice's income. Perhaps what Janice admires most about her husband is his "laid back" style. He never seems to get angry, he takes life as it comes. Most importantly he seems to enjoy his work and is a devoted husband.

During the final months of graduate school, Janice received at least a dozen telephone calls from universities and school districts inquiring about her availability for employment. Bob strongly encouraged her to pursue a career as a professor. Perhaps his urging reflected his own preferences and perceptions about work environments. Janice, however, had both a dream and a strong will—she wanted to be a school superintendent.

After mulling over four promising job opportunities, Janice accepted a position as a high school principal in a school only seven miles from the university. Bob was not thrilled because he knew the job would be stressful and require an inordinate amount of his wife's time. Yet, he was comforted by the fact that they would remain near the campus, an environment supportive of his writing and congruent with his easy life-style.

The principalship was challenging. Janice found time, however, to teach a course in school administration during the summer at her alma mater. Three years went by quickly. Janice's efforts as principal were rewarded by a promotion to assistant superintendent. This job brought new challenges and reinforced her dream to be a superintendent. In her second year in the central office position, she started to apply for superintendencies. But Janice was selective. First, she liked the western part of the United States and wanted to remain there. Second, she realized that some communities might not provide the resources that her husband desired for his profession. After three interviews, she received her first offer. The dream was near at hand.

The job offer came from Medsburg, the town where Janice grew up and where her parents still lived. This town of 19,000 was approximately 125 miles from their current residence. Two factors bothered Janice as she deliberated over the offer: (1) the effects of "going back home," and (2) Bob's willingness to move away from his many friends at the state university. Bob knew how much this job meant to his wife and told her,

"Listen, Medsburg College (a small liberal arts school) has a fine library. I can get by quite nicely there. We'll make new friends. As far as I'm concerned, you can decide. Either way it's okay with me." Janice decided to take the job.

It did not take long for Janice to regain her popularity in Medsburg. She knew many of the teachers and they were extremely friendly towards her. Janice joined the Chamber of Commerce, was appointed to the board of directors of the bank, and even won a citizenship award from her church. The school district prospered under her leadership. Janice was particularly adept at establishing coalitions to get things done. She believed in participatory management and involved parents, students, and teachers in many key decisions. She was even elected to the board of directors of the state superintendents' association. Things could not have been better.

One evening as Janice was relaxing and reading the newspaper, Bob called her from the kitchen.

"It's for you. Somebody named Anderson from Washington City." Janice picked up the phone in the den and said hello. She discovered that Anderson was Neal Anderson, president of the school board in Washington City, one of the largest cities in the state.

After identifying himself, Mr. Anderson continued:

"Dr. Melton, I got your name from Professor Berkowicz at the university. He told me you were a former student of his, and he went on to rave about your accomplishments as an educational leader. I called him because we dismissed our superintendent last night and we want to replace him as soon as possible."

Janice listened intently, occasionally injecting a "yes" or saying, "I understand."

"As you may know, Dr. Melton," he continued, "we are in the midst of a collective bargaining problem. In part, this situation led to the decision to terminate our superintendent. We want to hire someone immediately. We can't afford a year-long search or anything like that. That's why I called Henry Berkowicz, an old friend, and asked for several names of outstanding candidates. The board has agreed to invite the three persons he recommended. Obviously, you're one of the three."

"Well, Mr. Anderson," Janice responded, "I'm flattered. I really am. But I've only been in my current position for two years. My husband and I are just getting situated here; and to tell you the truth, we plan to stay here for a while."

The school board president answered, "I understand. But, Dr. Melton this is a rare opportunity. I don't know what your salary is in Medsburg, but I can assure you it will be a lot higher here. This is a good school district. Please, before you say no to an interview, think about it. Talk to your husband. If you interview for the job and don't change your mind, fine. We'll understand. But I think it is worth your while to examine this opportunity."

Janice talked to Bob and decided to interview with Washington City. The school board was most gracious and they were extremely impressed with her. A week after the interview, Janice was asked to return for a second interview and to bring Bob with her. The second encounter was more impressive than the first. Bob indicated how professional the board behaved and revealed he liked Washington City very much. When the offer was finally made, Janice almost fell out of her chair. It was not the offer, per se; it was the money. The total package amounted to 40 percent more than she was receiving in Medsburg. She accepted without hesitation.

The Washington City School District has a total enrollment of 45,500 students. Janice found herself with more central office staff than she had teachers in Medsburg. Collective bargaining was a perennial problem in the district. This year three issues became critical: (1) a 10 percent salary increase, (2) two hours per day of released time for building representatives to conduct union business, and (3) a payroll deduction plan for union dues.

On her first day as superintendent in the district, Neal Anderson sent her flowers and a note of congratulations. It read:

Janice,

Our board is totally committed to eradicating our problems with the teachers' union. This constant bickering and name calling has got to stop. It makes all of us look foolish. If you need to make changes, do so. If you need to step on toes, do so. We are behind you 100 percent.

Neal

About 75 percent of the administrative staff in the school district are individuals who acquired their current positions via internal promotions. A good number of them have never worked in another school district. The dismissal of Dr.

Bixler, Janice's predecessor, was an especially unpopular decision for this group because Dr. Bixler was "one of them." He had spent twenty-nine years in the Washington City system. Janice knew this when she accepted the superintendency; she also realized that there would be some resentment toward an "outsider"—let alone a "female outsider." In an effort to reduce such feelings, Janice immediately called a meeting of the entire administrative staff on arriving in Washington City. In a carefully prepared statement she outlined the following points:

1. The focus of her administration would be on the future, not the past. She was not interested in previous relationships, allegiances, and the like.
2. She expected that the administrative staff would function as a team. In order to accomplish this goal, mutual respect would be essential.
3. The first goal of her administration would be to resolve the current problems associated with collective bargaining.

Janice believed in confronting issues directly. During the second day in the superintendent's office in Washington City she called the teachers' union president, Malcolm DuMont, and asked to meet with the union leadership team within three days. Mr. DuMont was stunned. This had never happened before. Dr. Bixler rarely had any direct contact with collective bargaining or the teachers' union leadership. After receiving assurances that the purpose would be to share information, the union leader agreed to arrange the meeting.

In Washington City there are four assistant superintendents and a deputy superintendent. The person directing the collective bargaining process is David Zellers, assistant superintendent for personnel. He received a telephone call from Janice informing him of the forthcoming meeting. Zellers, one of the staunch supporters of the former superintendent, reacted negatively to this news.

"Dr. Melton, I think you're making a big mistake," he warned. "These people play hardball. The first thing they will do is to try to drive a wedge between you and the board's negotiating team. The rule around here has been that if they want to meet with someone from administration, they meet with me."

Janice responded calmly, "Well, it seems the current methods are not working very well. I want the union leadership to meet me. I want to assure them that I care about teachers. I want them to know that together we can build bridges. We simply cannot continue to exhaust our energy fighting each other."

"Am I going to be invited to this meeting?" Zellers asked.

"No," the superintendent responded, "I think it is best that this first meeting be rather informal. I don't want to give any indication that this is a quasi-bargaining session.

The meeting with union officials was held within one week and it lasted about one hour. The discussion focused mainly on the general condition of the school district, as Janice stipulated that she did not want to talk specifically about the current negotiations. The meeting ended with a request from Malcolm DuMont that Dr. Melton attend future collective bargaining sessions. Janice said she would consider his request.

The next morning, Janice arrived at her office at the usual 7:45 A.M. There, sitting in the middle of her desk, was an envelope marked "confidential." She opened it and read the contents:

Dear Dr. Melton:

Your recent meeting with the executive committee of the teachers' union is a matter that we find very disturbing. Fully accepting your authority to make such decisions, we respectfully urge you to discontinue direct interventions into collective bargaining. Your predecessor, Dr. Bixley, became a scapegoat.

He tried to convince our three relatively new board members that we must be firm with the union. These three individuals rejected his position, and they persuaded two of the four remaining board members to join them in dismissing Dr. Bixley.

The problems we are encountering are not new in Washington City. Most of us are former members of the teachers' union in this very district. We know how they operate.

We always have been able to bring collective bargaining to a successful conclusion and, given the opportunity, we will do so again. We cannot afford to have the union bosses running this school district. We urge you to direct your efforts to educating our novice board members rather than having direct discussions with the union's executive committee. There is no room for compromise with this group.

Respectfully,

David Zellers, Assistant Superintendent for Personnel
Alice Bontrager, Assistant Superintendent for Pupil Personnel Services
Duane Ibenhouse, Assistant Superintendent for Finance
Clyde Willis, Deputy Superintendent

Tom Zibick, the assistant superintendent for instruction, was the only high ranking administrator who did not sign the letter. Janice called him and asked if he knew about the letter. He said he did. She asked if he was requested to sign the letter, and he said he was. Anticipating her next question he said,

"I really don't want to discuss this action. I didn't sign it because I don't think such letters are appropriate and I also believe that a superintendent should be able to make critical decisions without being second-guessed by her staff."

Janice sat at her desk after the conversation. Her thoughts were like a roller coaster ranging from anger to concern. Was she being treated fairly? Did she have the right to make decisions about meeting with the union? Were her staff members correct in being critical of her behavior?

THE CHALLENGE: Place yourself in Janice's position. What would you do at this point?

KEY ISSUES/QUESTIONS:

1. Did Janice do the right thing in arranging a meeting with the union leadership?
2. How do personal values and beliefs affect one's perspective on collective bargaining?

3. List the advantages and disadvantages of Dr. Melton agreeing to do what four of her top five aides are asking.

4. Discuss the procedures under which Dr. Melton was employed. Given what you know about the district and its problems, was this a good procedure?

5. Evaluate the behavior of David Zellers.

6. If you were Janice Melton, would you share the letter with the board president (and the remainder of the board)?

7. Is it fair to generalize that individuals who acquired their current positions via internal promotions tend to behave in the same manner?

8. Assess Janice's leadership style of confronting issues directly.

9. In your opinion, was Janice Melton ready to be superintendent in such a complex school district?

10. Do you think the administrators who wrote the letter have a proper perspective of collective bargaining?

11. What are the possible advantages and disadvantages for Tom Zibick, the assistant superintendent who refused to sign the letter?

12. Administrators often rely on behaviors that have proven successful in past experiences. Is this a good practice?

SUGGESTED READINGS:

Blumberg, A. (1985). A superintendent must read the board's invisible job description. *American School Board Journal, 172,* 44–45.

Castetter, W. (1986). *The personnel function in educational administration* (4th ed.), chaps. 7,8. New York: Macmillan.

Cuban, L. (1985). Conflict and leadership in the superintendency. *Phi Delta Kappan, 67,* 28–30.

Darling, J., & Ishler, R. (1989/90). Strategic conflict resolution: A problem-oriented approach. *National Forum of Educational Administration and Supervision Journal, 7*(1), 87–103.

Forrest, J. (1984). The leadership team: Is the strategy working? *Thrust, 14*(1), 29–31.

Gonder, P. (1981). *Collective bargaining: Problems and solutions.* Arlington, VA: American Association of School Administrators.

Guthrie, J., & Reed, R. (1986). *Educational administration and policy,* chap. 12. Englewood Cliffs, NJ: Prentice-Hall.

Hanson, E. (1985). *Educational administration and organizational behavior* (2nd ed.). chap. 3. Boston: Allyn & Bacon.

Hirsch, P., & Andrews, J. (1984). Administrators' response to performance and value challenges: Stance, symbols, and behavior. In T. Sergiovanni & J. Corbally (Eds.), *Leadership and organizational culture,* pp. 171–185. Urbana, IL: University of Illinois Press.

Johnson, S. (1987). Can schools be reformed at the bargaining table. *Teachers College Record, 89,* 269–280.

Johnson, S. (1988). Unionism and collective bargaining in the public schools. In N. Boyan (Ed.), *Handbook of research on educational administration,* pp. 603–622. White Plains, NY: Longman.

Kerchner, C., & Mitchell, D. (1980). *The dynamics of public school collective bargaining and its impacts on governance, administration, and teaching*. Washington, DC: National Institute of Education.

Lieberman, M. (1984). Beware of these four fallacies of school system labor relations. *American School Board Journal, 171*(6), 33.

Lieberman, M. (1988). Professional ethics in public education: An autopsy. *Phi Delta Kappan, 70*(2), 159–160.

Perry, C. (1979). Teacher bargaining: The experience in nine systems. *Industrial and Labor Relations, 33*, 3–17.

Stuart, L., & Goldschmidt, S. (1985). *Collective bargaining in American public education: The first 25 years*. ERIC, Document Number ED271833.

Yukl, G. (1989). *Leadership in organizations* (2nd ed.), pp. 134–135. Englewood Cliffs, NJ: Prentice-Hall.

Who Will Censure This Board Member?

BACKGROUND DATA

The Richmond County School District covers 420 square miles. The district is predominantly rural and enrolls 7,800 pupils in two high schools, five middle schools, and ten elementary schools. The seven school board members are elected from designated geographic areas in the county to assure balanced representation among the twelve townships according to population data.

THE PROBLEM

Matthew Karman, the superintendent of schools, was driving down a lonely country road. The winds that came across the barren cornfields were icy. Although it was only mid-November, the chilling temperatures made it feel more like January. The fields were dotted with stalks severed about two inches above the ground. They looked like spikes someone had arranged to discourage trespassers. Mile after mile the stark scene was repeated.

After about thirty minutes of driving, Matthew pulled into the driveway beside a large three-story farmhouse. He was greeted by a german shepherd who fortunately was familiar with the educator. The barking summoned John Mosure from his barn. John was working on one of his tractors and had oil and grease all over his hands.

"I brought your board packet," Matthew said as the farmer waived in a sign of greeting.

117

Matthew ventures out one week before each board meeting and personally delivers materials to the board members. He feels it gives them ample time to prepare for the meetings and it gives him a chance to visit them on their "home turf."

"Come on in and we'll have a cup of coffee," John said, as he motioned to the superintendent to follow him into the house.

John Mosure is the president of the school board. He is serving his second three-year term, but this is the first time that he has been president. The two men are friends and work well together. On occasion, they interact socially.

"John, I hope you've got some time today. I want to take a couple of hours to discuss a sticky issue with you."

The board member responded, "Well, we'll just make time."

The two sat back warming their hands on the coffee cups and the superintendent started to share his concern.

"Two days ago, one of our high school principals, Bob Dailey at Polk High, received a telephone call from a friend in the state capital who is the assistant commissioner of the state high school athletic association. This friend asked Bob if he knew a person named Elmer Hodson."

John looked at the superintendent and said, "Oh no!"

Elmer Hodson was a school board member who constantly created problems.

The superintendent continued with his story, "So, Bob tells his friend that he knows Elmer and he tells him that Elmer's on our school board. This guy with the athletic association then tells Bob that Elmer's sitting in his outer office waiting to file a complaint against Bob and the football coach at Polk High."

"A complaint about what?" asked the board president.

"Well, Bob's friend didn't know at the time because he had not talked to Elmer yet. He just knew he was there to lodge a complaint against Bob and coach Yates (the head football coach at Polk High School). So he told Bob he was going to talk to Elmer and then call back before he did anything. About an hour later, Bob got another call from his friend. He said Elmer was upset about the fact that the quarterback at Polk no longer lived with his parents. It seems that this student, Jeb Boswell, is now living with the coach, Al Yates. So Elmer wants the athletic association to take action against Polk High School."

"Is there any merit to his charges?" John asked.

"First," the superintendent answered, "there is no question that the student is living with the coach. It seems that the boy's parents moved to Colorado this past June. The boy and the coach are pretty close, so Jeb asked his parents if it was okay to stay with coach Yates to finish his senior year because he wants to graduate from Polk. Coach Yates and his wife agreed to work something out with the boy's parents to cover his room and board. So, since about late June, Jeb has indeed been living in the Yates home."

"Can a student do that and still be eligible for athletics?"

"Well," the superintendent continued, "it seems that before this was done, coach Yates wrote a letter to the athletic association raising the same question. He was told that students whose parents moved out of the district could remain to finish their senior year without jeopardizing their eligibility so long as the parents and the school officials agreed to the arrangement. Bob Dailey and the parents both told coach Yates that they had no objections to the boy moving in with his family."

"So, Elmer doesn't have any complaint. What's the problem?"

"John, we have to put this in perspective. Here we are one week before the state play-offs in football. Polk has a nine and one record and is headed for the play-offs. Jeb Boswell is the star of the team, likely to make all-state or at least honorable mention. You know who the back-up quarterback on the team is?"

The board president said he had no idea. "You have to remember, Matt, that I don't live in the Polk area. I'm a South Richmond booster (the other high school in the district)."

"The second string quarterback is another senior named Ron Hodson."

The two looked at each other and smiled. The superintendent continued, "You got it, John. The second string quarterback is none other than the grandson of Elmer Hodson. Get the picture?"

"You know, I just remembered something," commented John. "You recall last summer when we were approving contracts for employing driver education teachers. Elmer made this big stink about coach Yates being a lousy driver education instructor. Do you think that was connected to this as well?"

"Who knows. With Elmer, it's hard to tell. But what's on my mind is what we do about Elmer. I think his going to the athletic association without informing the board or the administration was unethical. As a board member, he was in a position where he could have raised his concerns internally. He would've found out that there is no merit to his complaint. Further, he would not have embarrassed our school system before the officials of the high school athletic association."

"What did the fellow from the athletic association do about Elmer?"

"Nothing really. He explained that there was no violation and even told him that coach Yates had carefully asked for a clarification before agreeing to let Jeb move in with his family. Elmer accused the official of being corrupt and suggested that all of us educators were in bed together."

"So, why don't we just forget about this. Elmer is Elmer. He'll always be a pain in the behind. Why voters keep electing him is beyond me. Sometimes I think they enjoy all the trouble he stirs up."

The superintendent was not willing to let this matter slide. "John, we have to issue some type of reprimand to him. What he did was unethical for a school board member. I think you and the entire board should meet with him privately and issue a formal reprimand. Sometimes I think he believes he can get away with this stuff because people are amused with his behavior. I think this time we should put our foot down."

The board president got up to get the coffee pot and refilled the cups. He finished and sat in his chair. "How about if you put your foot down, Matt? You're experienced in dealing with people. I'm not. Wouldn't it be just as effective if you gave him the reprimand? We could ask the other board members how they feel about it. If they agree, and I think they will, you can tell him you are speaking for all of us. What do you say? Will you do it?"

THE CHALLENGE: Place yourself in the superintendent's position. Would you issue the reprimand or follow another course of action?

KEY ISSUES/QUESTIONS:

1. Do you believe that the superintendent is correct in his judgment that Elmer was acting unethically by going to the state athletic association with his complaint?
2. Survey school boards in your area and determine if they have policies related to censuring board members for unethical behavior.
3. Who should set standards for school board member behavior?
4. Do you believe that the superintendent was correct in taking this problem directly to the board president? Would it have been better to talk to Elmer first to get his side of the story?
5. Is it ethical or legal for school board members to vote on matters that affect members of their immediate families?
6. Is there an alternative to censuring the board member that the superintendent and board president should consider?
7. If you were superintendent, would you tell the media about Elmer's behavior? Why or why not?
8. Determine if your state has provisions for removing school board members from office. If so, what are these provisions?

SUGGESTED READINGS:

Banach, W. (1984). Communications and internal relations are problems for board members. *Journal of Educational Public Relations, 7*(3), 8–9.

Guthrie, J., & Reed, R. (1986). *Educational administration and policy,* pp. 48–55. Englewood Cliffs, NJ: Prentice-Hall.

Hamilton, D. (1987). Healing power: How your board can overcome the heartbreak of disharmony. *American School Board Journal, 174*(9), 36–37.

Hayden, J. (1987). Superintendent-board conflict: Working it out. *Education Digest, 52*(8), 11–13.

Institute for Educational Leadership (1986). *School boards: Strengthening grass roots leadership,* chaps. 8,9. Washington, DC: Institute for Educational Leadership.

Kowalski, T. (1981). Here's a plan for evaluating your board. *American School Board Journal, 168*(7), 23.

Kowalski, T. (1981). Why your board needs self-evaluation. *American School Board Journal, 168*(7), 21–22.

McDaniel, T. (1986). Learn these rarely written rules of effective board service. *American School Board Journal, 173*(5), 31–32.

Menzies, J. (1986). Power base preferences for resolving conflict: An educational management team consideration. *Journal of Rural and Small Schools, 1*(1), 6–9.

Myer, R. (1983). How to handle a board member who wants to play his own game. *American School Board Journal, 170*(11), 27–29.

Simon, T. (1986). *Fundamentals of school board membership*. ERIC, Document Number ED289232.

Wildman, L. (1987). *What can superintendents and board members do to help each other be successful?* ERIC, Document Number ED294312.

Woods, J. (1987). *Internal board of education conflict as compared to Coleman's theory of community conflict*. Unpublished Ed.D. thesis, University of Rochester.

CASE 18

Differing Perceptions of Teaching Effectiveness

THE COMMUNITY

Rio Del Mar is one of the Florida cities that is growing at an incredible rate. In the 1980s, the population increased from 62,450 to approximately 100,000. Located along the Atlantic Ocean, the city has attracted a number of high tech businesses. Real estate development is one of the primary areas of economic growth.

The city is also the seat of government for the county. There are two hospitals and eight banks in Rio Del Mar. Construction is taking place in all parts of the city. In addition to the public community college, there is a private liberal arts college located in the city.

The rapid growth in population has generated a number of problems for local government. The most serious relate to the environment. In the last five years, however, illegal drugs and related social ills have become at least equal concerns in the minds of taxpayers. A week does not pass without some major crime being reported in the city's daily newspaper.

The population growth in Rio Del Mar cannot go much further. The land within the city limits is rapidly approaching the level of 100 percent development. The impact of population increases, however, will be felt for at least the next two decades as areas surrounding the city are developed.

THE SCHOOL DISTRICT

The schools in Rio Del Mar are part of the county-wide school system. Growth is taking part in every sector of the county, thus the impact of population increases has been a special concern for the school system. At least one new school has been constructed each year during the 1980s; and in 1985, three new schools were opened. The challenge of population growth for facility planners in Florida is exemplified by the fact that recently Dade County (Miami) became the first school system in the United States to have a bond issue of $1 billion to support school construction. Although this county is substantially smaller than Dade, it still faces many of the same problems.

The school district is governed by a seven-member school board. The board members represent different geographic sections of the county. They are elected to four-year terms in nonpartisan elections.

With approximately 65,000 students in the school system, there are seventy-three attendance centers:

- 12 high schools
- 23 middle schools
- 37 elementary schools
- 1 alternative high school

The central office staff consists of over 100 professionals.

THE SUPERINTENDENT

Dr. Elizabeth Eddings is in her second year as the superintendent of the county school system. She came to this position after having served as the superintendent of a parish (county) school system in neighboring Louisiana.

During the interview process, which was conducted under Florida's famous "sunshine law," Elizabeth impressed teachers and administrators by candidly stating her opinions about the roles professionals should play in making instructional decisions. She is a believer in teacher empowerment.

Dr. Eddings is married to an accountant who recently relocated his CPA practice to Rio Del Mar. She is the mother of two children, Jason, a sophomore at Cornell University and Angie, a junior at one of the high schools in Rio Del Mar.

Elizabeth Eddings was born and raised in North Carolina. She is the oldest of five children. She started her teaching career after graduating from Western Carolina University in 1965. She completed her master's degree at the University of North Carolina in 1968. After three years of teaching and one year of experience as an assistant principal, she and her husband moved to Florida where she pursued her doctorate in educational leadership and her husband completed his master's degree and passed his CPA examination. Since completing the doctorate, Elizabeth has been an elementary school principal, assistant superintendent for instruction, and superintendent. She is active in several national organizations; and since accepting her current position, she has received a great deal of professional visibility.

THE SCHOOL

Seminole Elementary School is one of the thirteen schools in the district erected during the 1980s. It has five sections per grade level (six in kindergarten and first grade). Few of the teachers in the school have more than ten years of professional experience. The teachers in the school come from many parts of the United States, but most come from Florida and the southeast.

Seminole Elementary School serves one of the more affluent areas of Rio Del Mar. Included in its attendance boundaries are three of the most expensive subdivisions of the city.

The standard educational program in the school is augmented by specialized teachers in art, music, physical education, and computers (there is a teacher who operates the computer laboratory and provides instruction in this area). Additionally, the school has a full-time guidance counselor, a full-time assistant principal, and a half-time nurse and has access to the services of school district social workers and psychologists. There are three special education programs housed in the school: two classes for the learning disabled and a class for the mildly mentally handicapped.

THE PRINCIPAL

Howard Nissaum was employed as principal of Seminole Elementary School the year it opened. He was a fifth-grade teacher in another of the school district's elementary schools. Howard has had one of those rare opportunities to mold a new staff for a school.

The teachers, for the most part, are very positive about their principal. Howard is a "hands on" leader who likes to spend time in the classrooms. He works with teachers on instructional problems and occasionally does some direct teaching (about once a month, he will take a class in a teacher's absence instead of hiring a substitute). To create a schedule that permits interaction with teachers, Howard delegates much of the day-to-day administration to his assistant principal. These tasks include attendance, lunch programs, transportation, discipline, and supervision of record keeping.

THE TEACHER

Alicia Comstock is twenty-nine years old. She is in her second year of teaching at Seminole Elementary School. After graduating from a state university in West Virginia, she taught school at Richmond, Virginia, for three years before her husband was transferred to Florida by his employer.

Currently, Alicia is teaching a third-grade class of twenty-four students. This is a new assignment for her because all of her previous experience has been at the first-grade level.

Alicia is ideational and well-liked by her faculty peers. She is a positive person who rarely complains about anything. When you walk into her classroom, you feel welcome. You are fascinated by all the color and decorations. Her room is a warm and inviting environment.

THE PROBLEM

School district policy requires that principals evaluate every teacher annually. This assessment culminates with a formal conference between the evaluator and teacher sometime in mid to late March. Principals are obligated to follow policy guidelines that set time parameters and identify a standard instrument to be used. But, beyond these uniformity requirements, principals often exhibit different styles of administering performance evaluation.

Mr. Nissaum's approach to assessing teacher performance is to utilize the process in a formative manner. That is, he tries to make performance evaluation a positive growth experience for the teacher, students, and himself. His style is not one of confrontation. He believes that he must gain the confidence of his teachers in order to assist them in becoming more effective.

When Alicia Comstock was transferred to teach third grade, she accepted the assignment without complaint. But this was not an assignment that she necessarily wanted. Mr. Nissaum had an opportunity to hire an exceptional young lady who had just graduated from a university in the Midwest, but she would not accept the assignment at Seminole unless it was in the first grade. The principal thought it would be good for Alicia to have experience teaching at another grade level. So, given the restrictions for hiring the new teacher, he thought he could "kill two birds with one stone."

In early October, the principal received his first complaint regarding Mrs. Comstock. A mother called to voice a concern that her son was not being assigned homework. The principal responded by telling the mother that he would check into the matter but reminded her it was still relatively early in the school year. Within the next two days, the principal received two similar calls.

Collectively, these concerns prompted a conference with the teacher. During this meeting, Mrs. Comstock admitted to the principal that she was not a great believer in homework for students below the fifth grade.

"These children have a long school day and they work very hard at school. I just don't think much is accomplished by loading them with additional work to do at home," she told the principal.

The conference ended with an agreement that Mrs. Comstock would give some occasional assignments and communicate with parents more fully her practices with regard to homework. The tactic seemed to work because there were no more complaints for about six weeks.

In late November, the complaints about Mrs. Comstock resurfaced. This time, however, the dissatisfactions were broader than the issue of homework.

Parents were contending that expectations for academic progress set by the teacher were too low. As one father put it, "My son has never been happier about school. But why shouldn't he be? He's never had a teacher who let him do what he wants."

Principal Nissaum was now receiving formal letters rather than telephone calls from parents. Many indicated that copies were being sent to Dr. Eddings and members of the school board. Throughout this period, the principal apprised the teacher of the complaints and tried to work with her to resolve the problem. It was a most difficult situation for the principal, because he believed that Mrs. Comstock was an effective teacher. There was a problem, he judged, because many of the parents viewed school as having a very narrow mission (teaching basic skills). These parents were evaluating the teacher only on the basis of this one criterion.

In January just after the holiday break, the principal held a special meeting with the parents of students in Mrs. Comstock's class. All were invited to attend, even though only about one-half had been involved in filing complaints. Virtually all the parents who had voiced concerns came, but only about one-third of the others attended. The principal started the meeting by saying that he wanted to have positive things happen as a result of the meeting. He did not ask Mrs. Comstock to be present, he told the parents, because he did not think it would be productive at this point. The principal went on to explain his judgement that there was a difference in expectations between the teacher and some parents. The teacher viewed education as a process of dealing with the entire child. She was actually concerned about social adjustment, self-image, and educational progress. The complaining parents seemed to have a more narrow perspective, one that focused exclusively on skills and knowledge. This explanation was not well-received.

Benton Rodius, a stock broker, emerged as the spokesperson for the parental group—at least for the parents who were objecting to Mrs. Comstock.

"Mr. Nissaum, let me first say that I took a half day off from work to be here today with my wife. We obviously see this as a serious problem. Two years ago when we moved here from Vermont, I put my children in the public schools because I was told they were very good schools. My daughter, Betsy, who is now in Mrs. Comstock's class started going to a private preschool program when she was three years old. She could read by the time she entered kindergarten. I don't think its Mrs. Comstock's job to see that Betsy is happy. My wife and I take care of that. It is her job to challenge our child and to see that Betsy develops her skills. One of the things that is very wrong with public education is this notion that schools can solve all of society's problems. I pay taxes so my daughter can receive a fundamental education, not to have someone tinker with social values and decide whether my child is happy."

The principal reacted that he thought it was unfair to characterize Mrs. Comstock as someone who did not care about learning. He also noted that children come to a public school with a variety of needs and that the school had to be concerned with the total child. He further explained that academic, personal, and social needs could not be cleanly separated as distinct tasks.

After listening to the principal's explanation, Mr. Rodius asked the principal, "Well, what is your assessment of Mrs. Comstock?"

"It really would be inappropriate for me to discuss my formal evaluation of Mrs. Comstock with you. That process for this school year is not yet complete and will not be complete until late March. If you are asking me if I agree with the contention that she is not doing a good job, I can tell you in all honesty, I do not. Like all teachers, she can improve. I can become a better principal."

One parent interjected, "That's for sure."

The complaining parents were not satisfied with the principal's explanations and comments. Via their spokesperson, they made it clear that they were going to take the issue to the superintendent.

A similar meeting was held with the superintendent the following week. Dr. Eddings had lengthy conversations with the assistant superintendent for elementary education (Mr. Nissaum's immediate supervisor) and Mr. Nissaum prior to meeting with the parents. Fewer parents attended the meeting with the superintendent than had attended the previous meeting held at the school. Again Mr. Rodius served as the spokesperson for the group.

After listening for nearly two hours, Dr. Eddings responded to the complaints.

"It should come as no surprise to any of you that I talked extensively with my staff in preparation for this meeting. They briefed me on the nature of your complaints and after listening for the past two hours, I believe their assessment of your concerns is 100 percent accurate. Now, I'm not going to give you any lectures about how people have different expectations of public education. Time is too precious for that. I do want to ask you, the parents, to participate in a process that I think has a chance of resolving this conflict. I am convinced that Mrs. Comstock is a capable teacher. Also I believe that parents have a right to share in the process of setting educational expectations. What we need to do is to bring the parties together. Thus, I am suggesting a special committee that will work with this issue. The committee will consist of Mr. Nissaum, Mrs. Comstock, the assistant superintendent for elementary education, and one other teacher from Seminole Elementary School as well as four parents that you select to represent you. I want you to work to come up with a common set of expectations for Mrs. Comstock's class. Maybe after you listen to her perceptions about teaching and the needs of all students and after she listens to your concerns, we can find common ground. Now, I want to thank each of you for being here today. I believe that parental involvement in education is essential. Most importantly, I believe that we can take this conflict and use it to produce some positive outcomes. If we work together, if we take the time to understand our differences, I think we will become a stronger school district. Our children will be the beneficiaries of our efforts."

THE CHALLENGE: Assume the role of Mr. Nissaum in this case. Evaluate the decision of the superintendent and determine what you would do to carry out this directive.

KEY ISSUES/QUESTIONS:

1. Is it common for teachers and parents to have differing perceptions of what schools are to accomplish?
2. What factors determine a person's values and beliefs regarding public education?
3. Do you think that Mrs. Comstock's transfer to third grade is significant in this case?
4. Was it a good decision for the principal not to involve the teacher in the first conference with the parents?
5. Based on what you know from reading this case, do you believe that the principal shares the views of the teacher regarding what is important in education?
6. Could this problem have been averted by stronger interventions on the part of the principal following the initial complaints about homework?
7. What are the differences between formative and summative evaluation? Does the fact that the principal views the process as primarily formative have any bearing on this case?
8. Assess the superintendent's role in this matter. Was it good practice for her to meet directly with the parents? Should she have made a decision right there in the meeting?
9. Do you believe that the superintendent's support for the concept of teacher empowerment has any bearing on this case?
10. In what ways does the environment of the community affect this case?
11. What other alternatives could have been pursued by the superintendent in trying to resolve the conflict?
12. Is the superintendent correct in her assessment that conflict can lead to positive outcomes?
13. Evaluate the behavior of the principal in the January meeting he had with parents. Was he effective? What would you have done differently if you were in his place?

SUGGESTED READINGS:

Beckham, J. (1985). Legally sound criteria, processes, and procedures for the evaluation of public school professional employees. *Journal of Law and Education, 14*(4), 529–551.

Bullock, W., & Davis, J. (1985). Interpersonal factors that influence principals' ratings of teacher performance. *Planning and Changing, 16*(1), 3–11.

Castetter, W. (1986). *The personnel function in educational administration* (4th ed.), chap. 15. New York: Macmillan.

Epstein, J. (1985). A question of merit: Principals' and parents' evaluations of teachers. *Educational Researcher, 14*(7), 3–10.

Epstein, J. (1988). Parents and schools: How do we improve programs for parent involvement? *Educational Horizons, 66*(3), 59–95.

Glassman, N. (1985). Perceptions of school principals about their engagement in evaluation on the basis of student data. *Studies in Educational Evaluation, 11*(2), 231–236.

Margolis, H., & Tewel, K. (1988). Resolving conflict with parents: A guide for administrators. *NASSP Bulletin, 72*(506), 26–28.

Medley, D., & Coker, H. (1987). The accuracy of principals' judgements of teacher performance. *Journal of Educational Research, 80*(4), 242–247.

Medley, D., Coker, H., & Soar, R. (1984). *Measurement-based evaluation of teacher performance*, pp. 14–23. New York: Longman.

Minex, N. et al. (1986). *Development of a goal setting process and instrumentation for teachers and principals*. ERIC, Document Number 290796.

Moo, G. (1987). Communicating with the school publics. *NASSP Bulletin, 71*(501), 142–144.

Peterson, D. (1983). Legal and ethical issues of teacher evaluation: A research based approach. *Educational Research Quarterly, 7*(4), 6–16.

Redinger, L. (1988). *Evaluation: A means of improving teacher performance*. ERIC, Document Number 299231.

Ross, V. (1984). We use standardized student test scores to rate teachers. *Executive Educator, 6*(3), 22–23.

Sapone, C. (1982). Appraisal and evaluation systems: What are the perceptions of educators, board members? *NASSP Bulletin, 66*(458), 46–51.

Spillane, R. (1989). The changing principalship: A superintendent's perspective. *Principal, 68*(3), 19–20.

Snyder, K., & Anderson, R. (1986). *Managing productive schools: Toward an ecology*, chap. 8. Orlando, FL: Academic Press College Division.

Trentman, L. et al. (1985). Teacher efficacy and teacher competency ratings. *Psychology in the Schools, 22*(3), 343–352.

Wall, T. (1984). *The illusions of independence in evaluation*. ERIC, Document Number ED292831.

Wood, C., Nicholson, E., & Findley, D. (1985). *The secondary school principal* (2nd ed.), pp. 148–174. Boston: Allyn & Bacon.

Zirkel, P. (1985). Defamation for educator evaluation. *NASSP Bulletin, 69*(477), 90–92.

CASE 19

Trying to Prevent Unionization

Silatia lies in the heart of the "Bible Belt." It is a small city of about 55,000 that economically relies on timber and manufacturing. In some ways it is an isolated community. One must drive an hour and a half to get to a larger city. But many of the folks in Silatia do not worry about this distance. Most residents believe they have everything they need right in Silatia. There is a hospital, a small shopping mall, two movie theatres, a community college, and even a state park just outside of town.

Curtis James has been superintendent of schools in Silatia for about as long as anyone can remember. He is in his twenty-fourth year in that position. He recently told his staff of his intention to retire in two years. Some of his administrators do not think he really means it.

Curtis has experienced a great many changes in his tenure as superintendent of this school district of 7,300 students. Who would have thought twenty-five years ago, for example, that teachers would be bargaining with school boards? Yet this came to pass in Silatia about fifteen years ago, but not without tears, anger, and hard feelings. When the teachers first organized, Curtis took it as a personal insult. He saw himself as a friend of the teachers, a "father" who protected them from unreasonable taxpayers and unscrupulous board members. The onset of collective bargaining was a bitter pill for the superintendent to swallow. Nevertheless the process was enacted and now it seems its been in place forever.

"I told you fifteen years ago," the superintendent lectured his administrative staff, "that once we opened the gates to collective bargaining we wouldn't be able to control things. Well ladies and gentlemen, I was right."

Curtis was reacting to a petition he had just received signed by 85 percent of the nonteaching employees indicating that they have affiliated with the American

Federation of State, County, and Municipal Employees (AFSCME) and wanted recognition for bargaining purposes.

"The board members are going to faint when they see this. I tried to warn them years ago that this was coming. But no, they said teachers were different. The other employees will never want to join a union."

The leader of the movement to organize the Salatia School District employees is Vera Cobb, a secretary at one of the elementary schools. Vera is a widow who has worked for the school system for thirteen years. She does not care much for Superintendent James, and on several occasions told him so to his face. Four years ago, Vera was transferred involuntarily from the high school to an elementary school on the outskirts of town. The principal of the high school accused her of not maintaining confidentiality. The superintendent firmly believed that forming a union was Vera's way of getting even.

Curtis James held an executive session with his five school board members to discuss the petition from the AFSCME affiliate. All five members attended:

- Harold Huffman, factory worker
- Bobby Crokkit, farmer
- Duane Avker, foreman at the factory
- Lynn Murdrow, executive with the lumber company
- Stan Ullis, bank employee and president of the board

During his presentation to the board, Curtis could not restrict himself to the details; he inserted a good number of editorial comments. Not surprisingly, they were all negative toward unionization.

"Gentlemen, this is a Right-to-Work state. We don't want to recognize these people and my recommendation, plain and simple, is don't do it. You go ahead and tell them they can bargain and you'll have strikes, binding arbitration, and all other kinds of conflict before you know it."

Harold Huffman was the one board member who personally belonged to a labor union. The superintendent suspected that he would be sympathetic to recognizing the newly formed union. He was right.

"Curtis," Mr. Huffman responded, "you just don't like unions. The fact of the matter is that unions are here to stay. You think these folks are just going to fold up their tents and go away because you don't want to bargain with them?"

Stan Ullis, the board president chimed in, "Curtis, there isn't a whole lot to gain by fighting this thing. You know I don't want a union anymore than you do."

Curtis pushed his glasses back up the bridge of his nose and thought to himself that Stan was really worried that many of the employees were good bank customers and he did not want to do anything on the school board to make his boss mad. Again, Curtis was right.

As the discussion among the five board members continued that evening, it was evident to Curtis that at least three of the five were leaning toward recognizing the union. The support among board members seemed to strengthen his resolve that this union would not be recognized during his tenure as superintendent.

Over the years Curtis has amassed a large number of supporters in Silatia. He has provided many favors to patrons. He thought that he would have to put his own job on the line to repel the union recognition effort. If he could make the school board choose between him and the union, politically they would have to select him. Based on this strategy, he wrote the following letter to each of the board members:

Dear Board Member:

I have always campaigned against collective bargaining in education because I believe it is counterproductive. For the past fifteen years we have struggled with our teachers because of collective bargaining, and I think it has lessened the quality of our educational program while raising our costs. Now we are on the verge of approving collective bargaining for all of our employees. Some say I have been superintendent for too long. They're probably right. I plan to retire in two years. I'd like to leave this job with my head held high. But, I must tell you that if you recognize the AFSCME union, I'll resign immediately. Curtis James owes that to the people of Silatia. I don't want our citizens to think for one minute that I sold them out. I don't like ultimatums any more than you do. But from my perspective, there is no alternative. I once again urge you to say no to the union.

Respectfully,

Curtis James

The reactions of the five board members were mixed. The letter did not dissuade any of the three board members leaning toward recognizing the union. In fact, the communication angered Huffman and Ullis, who viewed the superintendent's attempts as "grandstanding." These two board members, along with Mr. Avker, met at Huffman's house to discuss the matter.

Huffman and Ullis developed a plan they thought would put the superintendent back on the defensive. Huffman explained it, "Curtis thinks he's got us over a barrel. Well, I think we ought to call his hand. You know he can't stand Vera, especially now that she's got this whole thing stirred up. Well she works for the youngest principal in the district, Mrs. Kendrick. Curtis doesn't like the principal any better than he likes Vera. I say we go talk to Mrs. Kendrick and see if she will agree to be the next superintendent. If she says yes, and I think she will, then we can tell Curtis that he can go ahead and resign. We'll tell him that Mrs. Kendrick will become the next superintendent. He'll be so mad, he'll forget all about the ultimatum he's given us."

The three sat there and giggled like schoolboys.

"You're right, Howard. We do this, and old Curtis won't know which way to turn," Stan Ullis said.

Duane Avker was the least enthusiastic about the plan. He voiced several concerns, "Hey guys, even though this plan is amusing, I'm not sure we should do it. First of all, how do we know that Mrs. Kendrick is the right person for the job? Second, how's the community going to react if they think we kicked Curtis out of his job when he only has two more years to retirement? Third, Curtis is apt to quit right away and his staff members, especially the ones in the central office, are so loyal to him, they might go too."

The three continued discussing the issue for another hour and the meeting culminated with an agreement that Howard Huffman and Stan Ullis would approach Mrs. Kendrick secretly to see if she would become acting superintendent in the event of Curtis's immediate resignation. That way, the board members could still conduct a search for a new superintendent and they would be covered if Curtis left office abruptly. The three further agreed that if Mrs. Kendrick agreed to become acting superintendent, they would vote to approve bargaining rights for the new union. If she refused, they would explore other options.

The two board members made an appointment to visit Mrs. Kendrick at her school. Behind a closed door, Mr. Huffman outlined the situation to the principal, but he did not tell her that their final decision regarding the bargaining matter would be affected by what she decided.

"Mrs. Kendrick, we need a good person to become acting superintendent if Curtis quits. We need someone we can trust. Who knows, you may like the job and we may like you and it could become a permanent situation."

"Does Mr. James know that you are here talking to me?" the principal asked.

"No," answered Ullis, "and he doesn't need to know."

THE CHALLENGE: Place yourself in Mrs. Kendrick's position. What answer would you give to the two board members?

KEY ISSUES/QUESTIONS:

1. Does the fact that Curtis has been superintendent a long time affect the way that you would react if you were Mrs. Kendrick?

2. Why do you believe Curtis is so opposed to collective bargaining?

3. What political dimensions affect the way in which school board members react to this request for collective bargaining rights?

4. Myron Lieberman argues that school board members do not always make good decisions related to collective bargaining because they can leave office to avoid the consequences of poor decisions. Do you agree or disagree with this judgement?

5. Assess the superintendent's strategy in sending the letter threatening resignation to the board. Was it ethical? Was it politically sound?

6. Assess the behavior of the three board members who met secretly at Huffman's house. Was it ethical? Was it politically sound?

7. What steps could be taken in this district to improve superintendent and school board relationships?

8. What factors should be weighed by the board in reaching a decision of whether to recognize the union for purposes of collective bargaining?

9. What is meant by "Right-to-Work State?" Are school boards in your state required to collectively bargain with all employees?

SUGGESTED READINGS:

Botan, H., & Frey, L. (1983). Do workers trust labor unions and their messages? *Communication Monographs, 50,* 233–244.

Castetter, W. (1986). *The personnel function in educational administration* (4th ed.), chap. 7. New York: Macmillan.

Goldschmidt, S., & Painter, S. (1988). Collective bargaining: A review of the literature. *Educational Administration Quarterly, 12*(1), 10–24.

Guthrie, J., & Reed, R. (1986). *Educational administration and policy,* chap. 12. Englewood Cliffs, NJ: Prentice-Hall.

Hanson, E. (1985). *Educational administration and organizational behavior* (2nd ed.), chap. 3. Boston: Allyn & Bacon.

Kearny, R. (1983). Public employment, public employer unions, and the 1980s. *School Library Media Quarterly, 11,* 269–278.

Kennedy, J. (1984). When collective bargaining first came to education: A superintendent's viewpoint. *Government Union Review, 5*(1), 14–26.

Kerchner, C. (1978). From Scopes to scope: The genetic mutation of the school control issue. *Educational Administration Quarterly, 14*(1), 64–79.

Kerchner, C., & Mitchell, D. (1980). *The dynamics of public school collective bargaining and its impacts on governance, administration, and teaching.* Washington, DC: National Institute of Education.

Kowalski, T. (1982). Organizational climate, conflict, and collective bargaining. *Contemporary Education, 54*(1), 27–30.

Lieberman, M. (1979). Eggs I have laid: Teacher bargaining reconsidered. *Phi Delta Kappan, 60,* 415–419.

Lieberman, M. (1984). Beware of these four common fallacies of school system labor relations. *American School Board Journal, 171*(6), 33.

Lieberman, M. (1986). Beyond public education, pp. 19–44. New York: Praeger.

Rebore, R. (1984). *A handbook for school board members,* chap. 10. Englewood Cliffs, NJ: Prentice-Hall.

Shedd, J. (1988). Collective bargaining, school reform, and management of school systems. *Educational Administrative Quarterly, 24*(4), 405–415.

Staw, B. (1984). Leadership and persistence. In T. Sergiovanni & J. Corbally (Eds.), *Leadership and organizational culture,* pp. 72–84. Urbana, IL: University of Illinois Press.

CASE 20

Let's Not Rap

Barb Doran was driving home from the airport listening to a popular AM radio talk show. It took less than one minute after tuning in for her to realize that she was the central figure in tonight's controversy.

Barb is principal of Roosevelt High School, a well-known secondary school located in a major city in Virginia. She has been at Roosevelt for less than two years. In that short period, she has established a reputation as a competent and forceful leader.

As she departed the airport parking lot and headed for the interstate that would take her to her office, she listened attentively as listeners called the program host to state their opinions.

"I think the principal should have the guts to cancel the program. We can't have groups coming into our schools when they symbolize hatred toward a group of people," a woman told the talk show host.

The next caller took a totally different position, "If the principal cancels this program, it just proves that there are still some serious racial problems at Roosevelt High."

As the show prepared to move to a commercial, the host commented, "Now, we're not taking sides here, but we'd like to hear from you about the 'rap' group that is scheduled to appear at Roosevelt High next week. Should Principal Doran let the program go on as scheduled or should she cancel it? That's tonight's question and it is a dandy. Call us at 555-2100 and let us know your opinion."

Barb was returning from a committee meeting in Orlando, Florida. She had only been gone two days and now returns to yet another controversy. During the commercial she thought to herself, "Why me, Lord?"

Roosevelt is a rather large high school enrolling 3,750 pupils. Most come from middle-class homes, but there are also wealthy and poor students. The school has a black enrollment of about 32 percent. The economic diversity among minority students is virtually the same as it is among white students. Roosevelt High School maintains an excellent academic reputation. In the past, it was frequently cited by state officials as a model school with regard to integration.

Since coming to Roosevelt, Barb has faced many problems, but perhaps the most difficult stem from the growing criticism emanating from a small group of black parents. They call themselves Parents Advocating Racial Awareness (PARA). PARA came into existence just prior to Barb's appointment as principal. The group's members were motivated by what they perceived to be a lack of sensitivity toward black culture and the black community on the part of the school's administration and faculty. Barb readily agreed to try to work with PARA and has been meeting with the group every five or six weeks in hopes of turning their energy into positive outcomes. The group contends that the school's racial problems were never publicized because black students kept quiet about the mistreatment and insensitivity they experienced. PARA has received a great deal of attention from the media, and among their continuing demands are the following:

1. an increase of black awareness in school activities
2. an increase in the number of black teachers and administrators
3. more emphasis on black studies in the curriculum.

About two weeks ago, Reginald Colter, a senior student, visited Barb. Reginald's father is one of the leaders of PARA and an attorney.

"Ms. Doran, don't you think we should do everything we can to send out messages about the dangers of drugs?" the student inquired.

"Absolutely," Barb answered.

"Well, my cousin in New York called last night and he said he could arrange for The Inner City to do a convocation at our school three weeks from now."

"What's The Inner City?" the principal asked.

"You don't know about The Inner City? It's a 'rap' group that makes records and videos. You probably have seen them on television and didn't even know it."

"Well, maybe I have. But what's this group got to do with discouraging drugs?"

The student showed the principal a promotional brochure about the group. "They're doing these drug prevention programs in schools as they go on tour to do concerts. These guys grew up in the ghetto and they know firsthand what it's like to use drugs as a teenager. They tell students that drugs will mess you up. So if we have them do a convocation, they'll do some of their rap, but the main purpose will be for them to discourage drug use."

After learning that the program would be virtually without cost to the school, the principal indicated that she would tentatively approve the project. She instructed the student to go see the assistant principal who handled the master schedule for the school. At the time, Barb did not give a great deal of thought to the student's suggestion. It was not uncommon for a high school the size of Roosevelt to have recording artists or professional athletes do student convocations.

The same day that Barb left for her committee meeting in Orlando, the concerns about the impending appearance of The Inner City at Roosevelt High began to surface. Students were informed about the convocation and a good number shared the information with their parents. The vast majority of parents reacted the same way that Barb did. They asked, "Who or what is The Inner City?"

There were some parents, primarily Jewish parents, who recognized the group immediately. It seems that one member of the group recently was accused of being anti-Semitic. The story appeared in one of those quasi-gossip magazines just about two months ago. During an interview with a reporter, this member of The Inner City talked about his views that Jews were largely responsible for oppressing blacks in the ghetto. He added that Jews were doing very little, in his opinion, to help blacks improve their standard of living. Additionally, this story examined some of the controversial lyrics on the group's records.

In forty-eight short hours, the issue of the impending convocation ballooned into a major controversy. Some of the parents who were concerned about the group's appearance at the high school contacted the newspaper. The reporter was delighted to do a story on the issue. The story appeared on the first page of the local section as follows:

ANOTHER CONTROVERSY AT ROOSEVELT

Some parents of Roosevelt High School students are objecting to a scheduled appearance at a school convocation of a rap group called "The Inner City" next week. The parents contend that at least one member of the group has made antisemitic statements to the press and that the lyrics of some of their songs are distasteful and not in the best interest of racial harmony. Principal Barb Doran is out of town and not available for comment. Assistant principal George Hampton said the group was scheduled to deliver an anti-drug message to the student body. He said he was unaware of any controversy surrounding the group before yesterday. Superintendent Paul Tolliver indicated he is looking into the matter and plans to talk with the principal when she returns to her office tomorrow.

The newspaper story led to the talk show that Barb now heard over the radio. Call after call was made to the station. The callers were pretty much evenly divided between those who thought the group should be allowed to appear and those who wanted the convocation cancelled. Barb did not know whether this division truly reflected public sentiment or whether the radio station was purposely trying to provide equal time to both sides.

Barb finally reached Roosevelt High about 7:30 P.M. All of the office staff had already left for the day. Only night classes and several athletic events required some persons to be in the building. She went to her office and quickly looked at some three dozen telephone messages. The majority related to the convocation. She quickly separated the messages into three stacks. The first group were those requiring immediate attention. The first message in the first pile was from Superintendent Tolliver. She called him at home.

"Barb, I'm glad you are back," he told the principal as he answered the phone. "Do you know what's going on with this convocation?"

"Well, I picked up the call-in show on the radio on my way in from the airport and that's how I learned of it."

"I tried to reach you in Orlando this afternoon but you had already checked out of the hotel. Listen, we have got to make a decision on this matter. The Jewish community is up in arms, demanding that we cancel the program. The black parents are threatening to take their case to the media if we cancel the program. They say a cancellation will just prove that blacks do not receive equal treatment at Roosevelt. Barb, this is a tough one!"

"Dr. Tolliver, do you have any strong feelings one way or the other? Even though this group may have a bad reputation in one area, they are coming to Roosevelt to give an anti-drug message. If they reach only one student and make a difference, don't you think it would be worth while to have them?"

There was a pause before the superintendent answered. "Barb, let's say this situation was reversed. Let's say it was a Jewish group that had been accused of being anti-black. Would you bring them into the school regardless of their purpose in coming?"

"Are you saying, Dr. Tolliver," asked Barb, "that we should cancel the program?"

"No, I'm not necessarily saying that. I'm just trying to point out all sides of this issue. I know you just got into town and you may want to talk to some of your staff before making a decision. I do think you need to make up your mind on this matter no later than noon tomorrow. Whatever you decide, I'll stand with you. I know it's not any easy decision, but it's one that is best made by you and your staff."

Barb reflected on the controversy. On the one hand, she thought about schools being a place for free speech—a place where varying views could be heard. Then she thought about the potential good that might come from having this group give an anti-drug message. But she also tried to put herself in the shoes of the Jewish parents. How would she react under the circumstances? Then she thought about what it would be like to be a black parent. The only conclusion that came easily was an affirmation of Dr. Tolliver's judgment—this is a "tough one."

THE CHALLENGE: Put yourself in Barb's place. What would you do as principal?

KEY ISSUES/QUESTIONS:

1. Do you think the principal should have handled this matter differently when approached by the student to have the convocation?
2. Do you think that the activities of the student's father had anything to do with the principal's behavior?

3. Should schools ever allow persons to speak to students if their views are contrary to the values and beliefs embraced by the community?

4. What are the advantages and disadvantages of cancelling the program?

5. What do you anticipate the repercussions will be if the program is cancelled?

6. Anticipate the repercussions if the program is not cancelled.

7. What are your impressions of Dr. Tolliver, the superintendent? Do you approve of his behavior in this case? What would you do differently if you were superintendent?

8. Prepare a statement that you would read or send to students announcing your decision (i.e., to either cancel or not cancel).

9. What is more important to a school like Roosevelt, fighting drugs or fighting racism?

SUGGESTED READINGS:

Drake, T., & Roe, W. (1986). *The principalship* (3rd ed.), chap. 7. New York: Macmillan.

Harker, R. (1981). *Multiculturalism and multicultural schools*. ERIC, Document Number ED225775.

Hollen, G. (1984). School assemblies as supplements to classroom learning. *NASSP Bulletin, 68*(472), 134–135.

Hoy, W., & Forsyth, P. (1986). *Effective supervision: Theory into practice*, chap. 7. New York: Random House.

Kowalczewski, P. (1982). Race and education: Racism, diversity, and inequality implications for multicultural education. *Oxford Review of Education, 8*(2), 145–161.

Margolis, H., & Tewel, K. (1988). Resolving conflict with parents: A guide for administrators. *NASSP Bulletin, 72*(506), 26–28.

McLeer, J. (1983). Understanding anti-semitism. *Curriculum Review, 22,* 99.

Pate, G. (1988). Research on reducing prejudice. *Social Education, 52,* 287–289.

Valverde, L. (1988). Principals creating better schools in minority communities. *Education and Urban Society, 2*(4), 319–326.

Valverde, L. (1988). Principals embracing cultural reality. *Teacher Education & Practice, 4*(1), 47–51.

Wood, C., Nicholson, E., & Findley, D. (1985). *The secondary school principal: Manager and supervisor* (2nd ed.), chap. 10. Boston: Allyn & Bacon.

Zirkel, P., & Gluckman, I. (1983). Stop, don't raise that curtain. *NASSP Bulletin, 67*(463), 110–112.

Who Decides Standards
for Employing a Principal?

School board meetings in Carrollton, an upper-middle-class suburb of a major city in Kansas, were once described in the newspaper as "downright boring." The board members like each other; the meetings are conducted with decorum; and the meetings rarely last longer than ninety minutes.

Adam Rieser has been superintendent of Carrollton School District for thirteen years. Prior to accepting this post, he was the assistant superintendent for business in the school system for five years. Dr. Rieser is the kind of person who never seems to get excited. He is personable and well-liked by most of the employees, especially the administrators. During Superintendent Rieser's tenure, the school district has grown from 5,300 students to nearly 9,000 students and has been involved in the construction of eight new schools and six other facility projects in which buildings were enlarged and/or renovated.

The school board in Carrollton is elected. Although there are usually many candidates seeking positions on the board, the elections are rather low-key affairs. This year seven candidates vied for two seats that would be vacated on July 1. One of the incumbents announced that he would not run for reelection and the other was being transferred by his employer to another community. The two winners of the election were Nadine Conchek, a librarian with the city library, and Karen McDougal, a certified public accountant. They were seated at the July board meeting and joined five veteran board members:

- Theodore Reller, account executive
- Matthew Packard, bank vice-president
- Kenneth O'Laughlin, engineer

- Susan Rustoldi, housewife and former teacher
- Donald Savage, English professor at a private university

Nadine and Karen adjusted well to the board, and their first six months were truly a learning experience.

In January, two of the district's seventeen principals announced they would be retiring at the end of the school year. This created two vacancies—one at the elementary school level and the other at the middle school level. Superintendent Rieser announced at the January meeting that the searches would commence immediately and that customary procedures would be followed. Board member McDougal confessed that she did not know the standard practices for filling administrative vacancies and asked to have the procedures described. The superintendent responded that such information would be sent to her within the next week. Mrs. McDougal was not satisfied with his response.

"I think that these are critical positions and the board, the faculty, and the public deserve to know the guidelines that will be used in filling the vacancies." Mrs. McDougal asserted.

The superintendent looked directly at Mr. Reller, the board president. The nonverbal cue was successful and the board president entered the discussion.

"You are absolutely right, Mrs. McDougal. Everyone has a right to know the ground rules for the searches. I don't think it is an efficient of our time, however, to discuss them here and now. Dr. Rieser indicated that he will forward a written copy of the procedures to you within a week. The staff in the school district will also be properly notified. I presume that we will follow the procedures that we have always used."

Superintendent Rieser nodded his head to confirm the board president's assumption. But Mrs. McDougal was still not satisfied,

"I'm not so much concerned about procedures as I am about the qualifications, the expectations. Who is going to decide what kind of persons we hire?"

Mr. Reller responded immediately.

"The board hires a superintendent and he employs his staff—subject to our approval, of course."

Mrs. McDougal was not going to give up.

"When Nadine and I were running for the school board, we met with a number of groups throughout our school district. For the most part, our patrons are very pleased with the schools in Carrollton. We heard, however, concerns voiced by teachers that the school board should expect principals to spend more time with instructional leadership and less time with management tasks. That is one reason why I'm asking about qualifications we desire for the persons who will fill these positions."

Nadine Conchek spoke next,

"That's absolutely correct. And I want to say that as one board member, I too would like to know about the guidelines relative to qualifications."

This type of discussion was very atypical for a school board meeting in Carrollton. It was starting to annoy board president Reller.

"With all due respect, ladies, the teachers don't run this school district. I am sure Superintendent Rieser will listen to their opinions. Those suggestions should be directed to him and not to individual members of the school board. Now, I want to say once again that there is nothing secret about the searches for the principals. Our job as board members is to set policy. Dr. Rieser's job is to run the school district. Now I suggest we get on with our agenda."

Board member Savage asked to be recognized.

"Ted, I'm not sure that this isn't a policy matter. I think the purpose of policy is to establish parameters for administrative decisions. If we decide that instructional leadership is an essential task for principals, then Dr. Rieser will be familiar with our expectations."

Knowing that the board president was becoming increasingly impatient with the conversation, Dr. Rieser interjected,

"Ladies and gentlemen, I and my staff welcome your direction regarding these searches. But let me remind you that it is I who should know what principals need to do; and it is I who should be recommending the parameters."

Mrs. McDougal responded, "Fine. What are the parameters you're recommending?"

"Mrs. McDougal," he answered, "we have used a standard set of qualifications for the last five or six principals we have employed. I do not have those documents with me this evening, but as I said earlier, I will send you a copy within a week."

"Well, Dr. Rieser, my problem is simply this. What if we do not agree with these qualifications? What if we want to change them? By the time next month's board meeting takes place, you may already have the announcements out about the positions."

Mr. Reller banged his gavel, something he rarely does, and declared that the conversation was out of order.

"How can it be out of order?" asked Professor Savage. "The item of the principalship is on the agenda and we have not voted on anything. In fact, I want to make a motion. I move that this matter be tabled until the February meeting and at least one week prior to that meeting we receive the superintendent's recommendation."

Mrs. Conchek quickly seconded the motion. Mr. Reller leaned over and conferred with the school board's attorney who was sitting next to him. The two whispered back and forth for about a minute and then the motion was ruled in order.

"Is there any discussion?" asked Mr. Reller.

"Yes." It was Mrs. McDougal again.

"I would like to request that Dr. Decker (the assistant superintendent for instruction) make an effort to talk to teachers in these two schools to hear what their views are regarding this matter. Then he can share that information with Dr. Rieser."

Mr. Packard, who had remained silent through the discussion, now asked to be recognized.

"This all seems so terribly inefficient. I'm sure our administrators have more important things to do than to conduct surveys regarding how everyone feels about hiring principals. I guess that's up to Dr. Rieser, though."

Again the board president asked if there was any more discussion. Mrs. Rustoldi raised her hand.

"I don't suppose it would hurt anything to see how key people felt about this. After all, teachers are the ones who are going to have to work with the principal day after day. You know, times are changing. Maybe we need to change too. Maybe the criteria that served us well five years ago aren't as effective today. I don't know. That's why I don't think it is a bad idea to have Dr. Decker talk to the teachers. But, that's just my opinion."

At that point, Mrs. McDougal called for the question. The vote was taken on Dr. Savage's motion to table the considerations regarding the searches for the two principals until the next board meeting. Voting in favor of the motion were Dr. Savage, Mrs. Concheck, Mrs. McDougal, and Mrs. Rustoldi. Voting against the motion were board members Reller, Packard, and O'Laughlin. The motion passed.

One of the reporters sitting in the audience leaned over and said to another reporter from the radio station, "This is more like it." The audience was stunned. In one evening the Carrollton school board had an open disagreement and a four to three vote. No one could remember the last time this had occurred.

THE CHALLENGE: Place yourself in the position of Dr. Rieser. What would you do regarding this matter?

KEY ISSUES/CHALLENGES:

1. Identify options available to the superintendent. Evaluate each.
2. Do you think it is good or bad that board meetings in Carrollton rarely last longer than ninety minutes?
3. Is it common for new school board members to challenge the status quo?
4. Should teachers have some input regarding the qualifications for principals in their school?
5. Should teachers ever be allowed to interview candidates for the principalship?
6. Do you think Mr. Reller, the board president, was trying to protect the superintendent?
7. How could this confrontation have been avoided?
8. Several board members view conflict as inefficient. Give some possible explanations for their judgment.
9. Do you think it is likely that this school board will now have split votes on many issues? Why or why not?

SUGGESTED READINGS:

Abbott, M., & Caracheo, F. (1988). Power, authority, and bureaucracy. In N. Boyan (Ed.), *Handbook of research on educational administration,* pp. 239–258. White Plains, NY: Longman.

Black, J., & English, F. (1986). *What they don't tell you in schools of education about school administration,* chap. 12. Lancaster, PA: Technomic.

Castetter, W. (1986). *The personnel function in educational administration* (4th ed.). chap. 9. New York: Macmillan.

Connelly, F., & Clandinin, D. (1984). *The role of teachers' personal practical knowledge in effecting board policy.* ERIC, Document Number ED271535.

Dow, I. (1983). The effect of school management patterns on organizational effectiveness. *Alberta Journal of Educational Research, 29*(1), 31–45.

Drake, T., & Roe, W. (1986). *The principalship* (3rd ed.), chap. 8. New York: Macmillan.

Fullen, M. (1983). *Change processes and strategies at the local level.* ERIC, Document Number ED245358.

Ibla, R. (1987). Defining the big principal—What schools and teachers want in their leaders. *NASSP Bulletin, 71*(500), 94–98.

Immegart, G. (1988). Leadership and leader behavior. In N. Boyan (Ed.), *Handbook of research on educational administration,* pp. 259–278. White Plains, NY: Longman.

Kaufman, R. (1983). A holistic planning model: A system approach for improving organizational effectiveness and impact. *Performance and Instruction, 22*(8), 3–12.

Lawler, E. (1985). Education, management style, and organizational effectiveness. *Personnel Psychology, 38*(1), 1–26.

Schon, D. (1983). *The reflective practitioner,* chaps. 1,2. New York: Basic Books.

Sloan, C., & Del-Bene, D. (1983). The perceptions of elementary school principals. *Journal of the Association for the Study of Perception, 18*(1), 11–14.

Trump, J. (1986). *What hinders or prevents secondary school principals from being instructional leaders?* ERIC, Document Number ED284365.

Wood, C., Nicholson, E., & Findley, D. (1985). *The secondary school principal: Manager and supervisor* (2nd ed.), chap. 9. Boston: Allyn & Bacon.

Yukl, G. (1989). *Leadership in organizations* (2nd ed.), pp. 22–23, chap. 3. Englewood Cliffs, NJ: Prentice-Hall.

CASE 22

"Narc" or Social Worker?
Or Maybe Educational Leader?

"Are you crazy?" Lowell Tatum asked his wife as the two were having dinner at their favorite restaurant in San Francisco.

"Now let me get this straight. You want to leave your nice job as coordinator of English education and become a high school principal. You ought to think about this—maybe for two or three years!"

Patricia Tatum has faced challenges all of her life; and with very few exceptions, she usually comes out the winner. Born in Los Angeles, she was the oldest of six children. Neither of her parents graduated from high school. All through school, she was a good student and a leader. In her senior year of high school, she received a scholarship to attend Loyola-Marymount University in California. By working two part-time jobs, she was able to make it through college, finishing in seven semesters and graduating cum laude.

During her college years, Pat worked as a teacher's aide in a parochial elementary school. It was there that she developed an interest in teaching. So after receiving her bachelor's degree in English, she accepted a position as a copy editor for a magazine only so she could take courses at UCLA at night to get her credentials to become a high school teacher. Eventually, she had to return to school full-time to complete the requirements; she was fortunately able to do this. During this two-year period, she met and married Dr. Lowell Tatum. At the time, Lowell was completing a residency in internal medicine at one of the hospitals in Los Angeles.

After finishing his residency, Pat's husband accepted an offer to join an established medical practice in the San Francisco area. Pat was employed in a teaching position at one of the suburban high schools. During the first five years of teaching, she managed to complete her master's degree and to have a baby. Lowell convinced his wife to take a leave of absence to spend time with the child for at least one year. The one-year absence from teaching stretched into six years and Pat had another child but kept taking university classes. Eventually, she accepted a fellowship and completed the residence requirement for her doctorate in education program.

At age thirty-four, Pat found herself with two children, a successful husband, and a newly acquired doctorate in education. She decided that she wanted to return to work and accepted a position as coordinator of English education for a large school district in the area. At first the job was exciting; but Pat soon found that she missed being around students. She shared this concern with her supervisor, Dr. Ernesto Javier, the associate superintendent for secondary education. He immediately offered Pat a new challenge—taking over the principalship of one of the high schools in the district.

When she told her husband at dinner that she wanted to accept the offer to become a high school principal, she got the reaction she expected. Lowell was not at all disturbed about Pat working outside the home, but he did not want her to take a job that would be overly taxing and stressful. Accordingly, the prospect of his wife becoming a high school principal was disconcerting. Yet, he knew that he could never persuade her to not do something once her mind was made up.

Western Valley High School was without a principal in December when Arlen Wadsworth suddenly resigned for health reasons. The three assistant principals at the school were all willing to take over, but Dr. Javier thought it was time for new ideas at the school. He believed any one of the assistants would be less likely to institute change than someone who had not been part of the administrative staff at the school. After weighing the various options, he recommended the appointment of Patricia Tatum.

Western Valley has 2,308 students in grades nine through twelve. The school population is diverse, from both an economic and racial standpoint. Most students come from middle-class homes and about 40 percent of the graduates go on to college.

As coordinator of English education, Pat had contact with the school and knew the teachers in the English department quite well. She considered them to be outstanding professionals and her previous experiences at this school were positive. On assuming the principalship, Pat candidly told her three assistant principals that she planned to devote most of her time to instructional leadership activities.

Over the course of the first four months in her new position, it became abundantly clear that Pat was not going to be able to fulfill her intentions relative to allocating her time. Most notably, the school was immersed in drug and alcohol problems. Although Pat was not totally unaware of this condition, she thought that her assistants would be able to handle discipline without much intervention from her. She quickly realized that she was wrong.

Pat's predecessor took a hard line toward substance abuse problems. Western Valley had one of the highest expulsion rates of any of the thirteen high schools in the district. The three assistant principals pretty much perpetuated procedures used by the former principal. The more Pat personally became immersed in discipline cases involving drugs and alcohol, the more she became convinced that existing actions were not effective. Yet, she did not exactly feel confident in this area given her limited experience with the problem.

Over the objections of her assistant principals, Pat established a committee to review the school's policies for dealing with substance abuse. She invited a parent who is a social worker and another who is a psychologist to join four teachers and an assistant principal on the committee. For two months, the committee mulled over mounds of data. After extensive review and discussion, the committee voted four to three to recommend the establishment of an in-school suspension program. Pat discussed the recommendation with her supervisor, Dr. Javier, before reaching a decision. He told her that the final decision was hers and praised her fortitude. But he failed to give specific direction. He merely commented that the in-school suspension idea might make a positive contribution. Pat decided to give the program a try. It would be established at the start of the next school year.

By October the in-school suspension program was bulging at the seams. Far more students became involved than the principal had anticipated. The program was creating more than management problems. Pat was receiving numerous complaints from parents and teachers. The following letter was somewhat typical of the parental concerns:

Dear Dr. Tatum:

It has come to my attention that students who are caught using drugs are being allowed to stay in school. As a parent, I think this sends the wrong message. My wife and I tell our children that using illegal drugs is a serious offense. I'm not sure that your approach to dealing with the problem reinforces our contention. I urge you to discontinue the in-school suspension program.

The issue of in-school suspension started to consume all of Pat's energy. She found herself devoting less and less time to her primary interest, working directly with teachers on instruction. The growing frustration became apparent to her husband.

"Pat, why don't you get out of this job. You don't need the grief. You are a good educator. You're not a social worker or a narcotics detective. Do what you were educated to do. Go back to your old job."

Pat knew that her husband's comments made a lot of sense. Yet, she did not like running from problems. Besides, her old job was no longer available.

There were mounting difficulties with the in-school suspension program. Two students already assigned to the program for possessing cocaine were arrested when undercover police caught them selling cocaine to other students in the parking lot. This incident was reported in the newspapers and the media had a field day with the practice of in-school suspension as a method for dealing with substance abuse problems.

A reporter on the local television show gave the following lead for his focused story on the student arrests:

In-school suspension at Western Valley. A solution or a part of the problem? Parents and teachers at Western Valley are up in arms over the continued use of an in-school suspension program instituted by Dr. Patricia Tatum, the principal. The concerns were heightened by the recent arrest of two students who were placed in this program and were later caught selling drugs in the school's parking lot. Officials in central administration said they are looking into the problem and did not want to comment at this time. Dr. Tatum said she thought it was critically important to keep these students in school and to offer them assistance. According to her, throwing them out into the streets is not the answer.

Pat received a call from the superintendent's secretary notifying her that she was to see the superintendent the next morning. Pat had only had three or four previous conversations with Superintendent Constantine since becoming a principal, and those encounters were all at social events. Dr. Nicholas Constantine does not meet with principals unless it is extremely important. During their meeting, he encouraged Pat to set firmer guidelines for allowing students to remain in school. He pointed out that the school district had an alternative school, a program for students not attending regular high schools. He also made it clear that he did not want all of the controversy to continue.

When Pat returned to her office, she met with the assistant principals. They too encouraged her to discontinue the in-school suspension program. Down deep, Pat knew that the program had helped some students. But no one wanted to talk about the successes. Two days later Pat received an anonymous letter that was more stinging than any of the previous complaints. The letter contended that Pat was incompetent and being protected because she was a black female. The letter was written on Western Valley High School stationery.

Pat started to doubt her own abilities. She knew that other high schools had tried in-school suspension programs and they did not have this type of trouble. Why was Western Valley having so much trouble? Maybe her detractors were correct. Pat called Dr. Javier and asked for an appointment. During their meeting, Pat admitted having self-doubts and requested counsel. Dr. Javier found it difficult to respond.

"Pat, I probably am to blame for getting you into this job. If you are unhappy, maybe you should get out. But if you're considering leaving just because of the in-school suspension issue, I think you're making a mistake. If it's not drug problems, it will be something else. That's the life of a high school principal. If you decide you want out of Western Hills, I'll find you a job back here in our division. You think about it. Discuss it with your husband. Make the decision on what you think is best for your career. Don't let this one problem deter your goals."

THE CHALLENGE: Place yourself in Pat's position. What would you do?

KEY ISSUES/QUESTIONS:

1. Do you think Pat was prepared to become principal of this school? Why or why not?

2. Was it a good idea to appoint a committee to recommend what should be done about substance abuse problems?
3. What is your impression of the behavior of the three assistant principals in this case?
4. Do you think that Pat's family situation has any bearing on this case? If so, in what respect?
5. What are the advantages and disadvantages of in-school suspension programs?
6. Is the size of the school an important consideration in this case?
7. Do you think Dr. Javier gave Pat good advice?
8. What alternatives could Pat have pursued instead of the in-school suspension program?
9. Do you think school administrators receive adequate academic preparation to deal with problems such as the one in this case?
10. Do you think the school district should have specific policies governing the operation of in-school suspension programs?
11. Do you think that women face special problems in the secondary principalship?

SUGGESTED READINGS:

Buscemi, M. (1985). What schools are doing to prevent alcohol and drug abuse. *The School Administrator, 4*(9), 11–14.

Daria, R. (1987). Remedy for drug abuse: Honesty, discipline, help for troubled students. *American School Board Journal, 174*(8), 37, 54.

Edson, S. (1981). *Female aspirants to public school administration: Why do they continue to aspire to principalships?* Unpublished Ed.D. thesis, University of Oregon.

Erickson, H. (1985). Conflict and the female principal. *Phi Delta Kappan, 67*(4), 288–291.

Farmer, N. (1983). *Characteristics of women principals in North Carolina.* Unpublished Ed.D. thesis, University of North Carolina, Chapel Hill.

Farrar, E., & Hampel, R. (1987). Social services in American high schools. *Phi Delta Kappan, 69*(4), 297–303.

Fertman, C., & Toca, O. (1989). A drug and alcohol aftercare service: Linking adolescents, families, and schools. *Journal of Alcohol and Drug Education, 34*(2), 46–53.

Heron, B. (1988). Eliminating drug abuse among students. *Clearing House, 61,* 215–216.

Knoff, H. (1983). Solving school discipline problems: Look before you leap. *Clearing House, 57,* 155–157.

Lewis, J. et al. (1987). *Drug and alcohol abuse in the schools: A practical policy guide for administrators and teachers on how to combat drugs and alcohol.* ERIC, Document Number ED281304.

Lohrmann, D., & Fors, S. (1988). Can school based educational programs really be expected to solve the adolescent drug abuse problem? *Journal of Drug Education, 18,* 327–338.

Malvin, J. et al. (1985). Evaluation of two school-based alternatives programs. *Journal of Alcohol and Drug Education, 30*(3), 98–108.

Rosiak, J. (1987). Effective learning demands drug-free schools. *NASSP Bulletin, 71*(497), 128–133.

Sawyer, K. (1984). *The right to safe schools: A newly recognized inalienable right.* ERIC, Document Number ED253966.

Shea, L. (1984). *Women and the high school principalship: A comparison of male and female aspirations and career paths.* Unpublished Ed.D. thesis, Lehigh University.

Sheppard, M. (1984). Drug abuse prevention education: What is realistic for schools? *Journal of Drug Education, 14*(4), 323–329.

Sullivan, J. (1988). *A study of the evolution of three inschool suspension programs in Virginia.* Unpublished Ed.D. thesis, College of William and Mary.

Sullivan, J. (1989). Elements of a successful in-school suspension program. *NASSP Bulletin, 73*(516), 32–38.

Washington, P. (1986). *A study of administrator and teacher perception and attitude toward inschool suspension programs at selected high schools of the metropolitan St. Louis school districts.* Unpublished Ph.D. thesis, Saint Louis University.

Watson, D., & Bright, A. (1988). So you caught them using drugs: Now what? *Thrust, 17*(3), 34–36.

Zorn, R. (1988). New alternatives to student suspensions for substance abuse. *American Secondary Education, 17*(2), 30–32.

CASE 23

Never, Never, Never Try to Get in the Taxpayer's Pocket

In 1973, Indiana passed a law that is commonly known as the "Tax Freeze Law." This statute covers all governmental units, but it treats school districts more harshly than other public taxing agencies. The tax levies of school districts were frozen whereas the tax rates of other agencies were kept in place. The net effect is increasing assessed valuations of school districts and simultaneously declining tax rates. By contrast, frozen tax rates permit cities and other governmental units to utilize additional revenues stemming from increases in the assessed valuation.

The intention of the Indiana law was to lessen the burden on the property tax for supporting public agencies. At the time the law was passed, about two-thirds of the revenues for local school districts came from local taxes. Today, the rate is more like one-third. Thus, as less revenues were received from local taxes, state support was increased.

Many superintendents in Indiana do not agree that the increased support from the state has been sufficient to offset the loss in local revenues. One of those superintendents is Terrance Severta. Terry is top administrator in Eastern Boswell County, a rural school district located in east central Indiana. In many ways, Eastern Boswell has had the worst of all conditions. Prior to the tax freeze program, the teacher salaries in the district ranked 241st out of 309 school districts. The assessed valuation per pupil in the district was also below the state average. In the seventeen years since the freeze has been in effect, the district has lost about 15 percent of its enrollment (due largely to declining birth rates and some out-migration).

The school district is composed of six rural townships. There are two or three small towns within the school district's boundaries, but each town does not amount to much more than a grain elevator and grocery store. There are three schools in the district: a junior/senior high school and two elementary schools. The total enrollment is 1,367 pupils.

Two years ago when the school board employed Terry Severta, they had just experienced a bitter teachers' strike. The board was so angered over the way the matter was handled by the school district's administration that the members voted to dismiss the superintendent and one of the principals. The school board openly told the community that it never wanted to have another strike. The board members selected Terry because they perceived him to be a good-natured person who could get along with almost everyone. Contacts with persons who had worked with Terry indicated that he was a pleasant person who was always willing to look at both sides of an issue.

The central office staff in the school district consists of the superintendent, a director of transportation, two secretaries, and a bookkeeper. Terry appreciates the hard work and support of each one of his staff members. During the past several months, he found himself spending an unusual amount of time with Mrs. Hatcher, the bookkeeper. The superintendent was trying to find some resources to improve programming in the district. One of the problems confronting small, rural school districts is the ability to add programs in an effort to keep pace with larger school systems. The specific additions that the superintendent desired were the following:

1. a counselor for the two elementary schools
2. a full-time librarian for the elementary schools
3. a second nurse for the school district
4. computer labs for all of the schools.

Terry also wanted to raise funds to increase employee salaries by 15 percent over the next two years. His goal was to take the salaries to the state average.

His consultation with Mrs. Hatcher was informative but failed to provide a solution for his financial needs. As Mrs. Hatcher told him, "You just can't get blood out of rock." Indeed, what the superintendent found as he scrutinized the fiscal data of the school system was not the added funds he desired, but rather strong indications that the school district may have to cut programs to remain solvent.

Superintendent Severta arranged a luncheon meeting with his board president, John Oberdorfer, to discuss the matter. John is a farmer and is well-respected in the community.

"John," Terry began, "we have got some real money problems. I've been going over our financial data carefully. I started out hoping to find some dollars to add the programs I suggested we needed to keep pace with other school systems. What I found was something very different."

The board president listened attentively. Then he asked,

"Isn't there some way we can raise added dollars?"

Terry responded, "There is only one way. Under the tax freeze program we can hold a referendum to increase tax rates. It's the only way."

John smiled and said, "And what do you think our chances will be? No one's too fond of property taxes, you know."

The meeting between the superintendent and board president ended on a small note of encouragement.

"I'll tell you this, Terry. If you reach the decision to move forward with this, and provided the tax increase would be modest, I'll do everything I can to convince the other four board members to support having a referendum. That's the best I can do."

After the meeting with John Oberdorfer, Terry decided that he would also meet with Francine Turner, the president of the teachers' association. The two have developed a good relationship. Francine believes that Terry wants to do things to improve the quality of education in the school system. After listening to his concerns, she agreed that the referendum was needed. She encouraged the superintendent to move forward and pledged that the teachers' association would back the initiative to the hilt.

Prior to coming to Eastern Boswell County, Terry was an assistant superinten-dent in a larger school district in the southern part of the state. He called his former boss, Dr. Ernie Butler, and asked if the two could meet in Indianapolis. Dr. Butler was happy to oblige his former aide. Terry made a second appointment in conjunction with his trip to the state capital. That appointment was with his local state senator, Senator Tiles, a member of the Senate Education Committee.

In preparing for the two appointments in Indianapolis, Terry reviewed a number of articles about referenda. He was struck by the divergence of opinions in the literature. For example, one writer indicated that a positive approach should be taken in attempting to pass a referendum—one that emphasizes the good things that will occur if the added revenues are obtained. Another article suggested that you should tell the taxpayers what they will lose if the referendum fails. This latter article further indicated that it is helpful if cuts in athletic programs are among the items publicized. Although these position papers were informative, they in no way gave Terry clear direction.

In Indianapolis, Terry first met with his former boss, Dr. Butler. The two had a late breakfast at one of the hotels located across the street from the Capitol Build-ing. Terry started the conversation by stating that he was seeking advice. He told Dr. Butler about the financial problems in his district and shared with him the various materials he had read in professional journals on the topic of referenda. He asked his former boss what he would do if he were superintendent of Eastern Boswell County.

"Terry, let me tell you something. You never, never, never try to get in a taxpayer's wallet. You can close schools, and your patrons eventually get over it. You can curtail programs, and they learn to manage. But you raise their taxes, and they never forget it. Besides, you probably don't have much of a chance of passing a tax increase referendum in that school district anyway. Why take the risk?"

After a meeting that lasted about two hours, Terry walked across the street for his 11:15 A.M. appointment with Senator Tiles. In the two years he has been in Eastern Boswell County, Terry has gotten to know the senator who is considered a powerful person on the Senate Education Committee. He was greeted warmly by his host when he arrived.

For a second time that morning, Terry outlined the financial problems in his school district, and again he asked for advice.

"Terry, the referendum was never really designed to be a method to allow local school districts to raise additional money. Sure, the option is there; but legislators have never tried to pass the method off as a viable alternative for additional funding. Just look at the failure rate of these initiatives in this state. I think it's something like three to one. That ought to tell you something."

Terry then asked if there was any hope that the state legislature would do something in the near future to increase funding for schools.

The senator answered, "It's not likely. The state isn't exactly in the best financial shape. The tax freeze program was passed because legislators knew that people were fed up with the property tax. There are an awful lot of elected officials in this town who are not convinced that more money is the answer to better education—and I am one of them. My advice is to look closely at areas where you can fine tune the budget. If you make cuts and the people are unhappy, maybe they'll suggest a referendum. That way, your chances of passing the thing are a lot greater."

As he drove back from Indianapolis, Terry concentrated on the advice he had been given. Both individuals essentially told him to forget about the referendum. Terry kept asking himself why he wasn't convinced. He truly believed that the programs and salary increases were needed and that he only had one option to obtain these resources. He was torn between the practical, political advice he just received and the considerations that he believed were the responsibility of an educational leader.

Terry decided that there was one more person with whom he should speak. On his way back from Indianapolis, he made a detour to visit one of his former professors, Dr. Vicki Tallimore. Professor Tallimore teaches courses in policy development and collective bargaining at one of the state universities. She is known as an excellent teacher, and Terry admires her ability to understand complex problems. He found her in her office meeting with a student. He waited outside the door until she was finished.

Dr. Tallimore was pleased to see her former student and the two spent about fifteen minutes recapping their lives since they last saw each other. Then the discussion turned to the problem that was consuming the superintendent. Professor Tallimore listened attentively and responded.

"Terry, I think you have a moral obligation to move forward with this referendum. You don't write the rules. You didn't put the tax freeze in place. You have to work with the tools that are available; and like it or not, the referendum is the only option that you have. You are the educational leader of your school system. You have to be the one who reminds the community that there are financial obligations related to public education in a democratic society. Besides, you can't turn your back on the teachers now. You already told the union president that you were considering the referendum. They will think more of you as a leader even if the initiative fails."

Terry suspected that Professor Tallimore would offer a perspective to this problem that would be different from what he heard earlier that day. Her comments made him agonize all the more over what to do. When he returned to his office it was well past 6:00 P.M. and the offices were empty. He turned on his light and sat at his desk writing out some key questions he knew he had to answer:

1. How will the board react if he recommends a referendum? Will they support it?
2. How will the teachers react if he does not move forward?
3. What programs will they have to cut if they do not get additional funds?
4. What are the chances of a referendum passing?

The more he wrote, the more discouraged he became. Around 8:00 P.M. he called his wife and told her he would be home in ten minutes.

THE CHALLENGE: Place yourself in Terry's position. What would you do at this point?

KEY ISSUES/QUESTIONS:

1. Outline the different effects of a frozen tax rate versus a frozen tax levy. Why are the schools at a disadvantage because they have a frozen levy?
2. Did the superintendent do the right thing when he met with the president of the teachers' association and told her he was considering asking for a referendum?
3. Why does the literature offer differing opinions about referenda? Should there be a set of principles that are best to follow?
4. Why do so many taxpayers and elected officials believe that schools are inefficient organizations?
5. Is Superintendent Severta looking in the right place for information? Would you have looked elsewhere for information and advice?
6. If you were the superintendent, would you believe the board president when he says he will do what he can to get the other four board members to approve the referendum?
7. How do you interpret Senator Tiles's comments that "the referendum was never intended to be a viable alternative for raising additional funds?"
8. React to the advice that Terry received from his former boss? Is Dr. Butler right? What leads you to agree or disagree with his advice?
9. Is it common for superintendents to face situations where political and professional considerations are in conflict? Is this more or less true in other professions (e.g., law, medicine)?

SUGGESTED READINGS:

Banicki, G. (1987). *The study of potential voter behavior to an educational tax referendum.* Unpublished Ed.D. thesis, Northern Illinois University.

Black, J., & English, F. (1986). *What they don't tell you in schools of education about school administration*, chap. 16. Lancaster, PA: Technomic.

Chopra, R. (1988). How we passed a bond issue hard on the heels of a tax hike. *American School Board Journal, 176*(6), 26, 29.

Clodi, D. (1987). *The relationship between educational tax rate referendum outcome and both campaign strategies and selected demographic variables*. Unpublished Ed.D. thesis, Illinois State University.

Dana, J. (1985). *A field study of voter behavior in school bond election failures*. Unpublished Ph.D. thesis, University of Missouri, Columbia.

First, P. (1986). Here's how press coverage can boost (or bust) your next school referendum. *American School Board Journal, 173*(11), 42.

Guthrie, J., Garms, W., & Pierce, L. (1988). *School finance and public policy* (2nd ed.), chap. 5. Englewood Cliffs, NJ: Prentice-Hall.

Hahn, H., & Kamieniecki, S. (1987). *Referendum voting*, pp. 119–131. New York: Greenwood Press.

Hamel, G. (1984). Fairfax county loves its schools. *School Business Affairs, 50*(2), 32, 50.

Henry, J. (1987). Help for passing bond referenda. *School Business Affairs, 53*(12), 26–27.

Humphrey, S., & Weber, J. (1985). Why finance elections fail: Passive referendum campaigns are no longer effective. *Journal of Educational Public Relations, 8*(3), 30–33.

Kaiser, H., & Nelson, G. (1982). Inequality and the Minnesota referendum levy. *Journal of Education Finance, 8*(2), 152–169.

Ornstein, A. (1989). Trimming the fat, stretching the meat for the 1990s budgets. *The School Administrator, 9*(46), 20–21.

Ross, V. (1983). Don't be daunted by defeat: Score a bond issue victory. *Executive Educator, 5*(4), 25–26.

Walker, B. (1984). The local property tax for public schools: Some historical perspectives. *Journal of Education Finance, 9*(3), 265–288.

CASE 24

The Clinic Controversy

THE COMMUNITY

Shelton is a city of 90,000 residents. The population of the community exemplifies the "melting pot" nature of industrial sections of the United States. Shelton is a manufacturing town in the mideast. Unlike similar cities, it has not suffered significantly in the areas of population decline or economic vitality.

The primary industries in Shelton include the following:

- Truck trail factory, 950 employees
- Wire factory, 840 employees
- Automobile ignition plant, 560 employees
- Lawnmower assembly plant, 400 employees

Jobs remain plentiful in the city, and since the 1980 census, the population has increased by 10 percent. Industry in Shelton is highly unionized. Salaries for assembly line jobs are quite high. Starting salaries for unskilled labor range from $5.80 to $8.20 per hour.

The community is composed of ethnic neighborhoods. Many of the residents are of Italian descent. In recent years, the black and Hispanic populations have been growing rapidly. Currently, official populations statistics for the city list the following:

- White—59 percent
- Black—31 percent
- Hispanic—8 percent

- Native American—1 percent
- Other—1 percent

The city has its own hospital and a relatively new shopping center. The downtown area, however, is slowly fading away. Most stores have relocated or have gone out of business. Railroad tracks cross through Shelton in every direction. Being stopped by freight trains is a common occurrence as the residents drive through the city.

THE SCHOOL DISTRICT

The Shelton City School District is one of four school systems in Parma County. Statistics for the district are as follows:

- High schools: 4
- Middle schools: 9
- Elementary schools: 26
- Current enrollment: 24,900

The superintendent is Dr. Fredrick Ochman, a veteran administrator in his sixth year as the chief executive of this district. Prior to coming to Shelton, Dr. Ochman served as superintendent in two smaller districts in two different states. He is perceived by his staff to be a "hands on" leader who likes to get involved with key issues.

The central office staff includes fourteen professional staff members. There are three assistant superintendents who report directly to Dr. Ochman:

- James Effrin, assistant superintendent for business
- Lucy Natali, assistant superintendent for pupil personnel services
- Richard King, assistant superintendent for instruction

The school district is governed by a seven-member board. Just three years ago the method for selecting board members was changed from appointments being made by the mayor to members being elected. Only two of the members who were in office when Dr. Ochman was originally appointed superintendent remain on the school board.

THE PROBLEM

There have been many accomplishments for the Shelton City School District. The schools have won their fair share of awards for both academics and athletics. In reviewing data annually as part of the strategic planning process, Superintendent

Ochman became alarmed by the continuing increase in the drop-out rate. There were two dimensions of this issue that were especially troublesome: (1) the rate had increased most markedly among female students, and (2) the rate was increasing most rapidly among those students who resided in the lower socioeconomic areas.

Dr. Ochman established an ad hoc committee to explore the problem of drop outs in detail. He assigned Dr. Natali the task of chairing the committee that consisted of three administrators, six teachers, four parents, and four students. After studying relevant information for nearly six months, and after retaining a consultant to assist in the analysis, Dr. Natali issued a written report on behalf of the committee. Among the more cogent conclusions were the following:

1. The existence of low skill jobs in the community and surrounding areas continues to tempt students to leave school prematurely. This is especially true for male students.
2. Most students who drop out of school come from homes where there is a low level of support for education. Often the student's have one or two parents who did not complete high school.
3. Corresponding with the increase in the drop-out rate has been an increase in the pregnancy rate among students. Students involved in a pregnancy are five times more likely to drop out than those who are not pregnant.
4. There is a rather high correlation between low family income and student pregnancy. Students living in families below the poverty level are six times more likely to become pregnant.
5. Most students involved in a pregnancy have had virtually no consultation, sex education, or health care.

After studying the report for more than a month, Dr. Ochman held a series of meetings with his administrative staff to discuss the matter. He was especially interested in hearing what the building principals had to say about the data (i.e., did they agree with them) and what they had to offer in the way of suggested courses of action. The principals did not challenge the data; but there were distinctive differences in their suggested solutions. Some principals took the "hard line" approach, advocating that schools were for learning and not all adolescents belonged there. At the other end of the spectrum, there were principals who believed that the schools were the best hope for salvaging some of these students.

Following the review and discussions with administrative staff, Dr. Ochman invited nine community leaders to meet with him to further explore the problem of drop outs. These leaders included the mayor, the administrator of the hospital, the director of the mental health clinic, a priest, a minister, a rabbi, a physician, the director of the local family planning agency, and the president of the school board. As with his administrative staff, Dr. Ochman encountered little disagreement regarding the accuracy of the data collected and the conclusions drawn by the ad hoc committee. But again, there were significant differences among the participants regarding courses of action. One of the positive outcomes that emerged from the meeting with community leaders was the revelation that little was being done to coordinate community resources to address the problem.

In deliberating potential solutions, Superintendent Ochman arrived at several conclusions:

1. No single course of action would suffice. There were several major reasons why students dropped out of school and each needed to be treated separately.
2. That to have any success in curtailing the drop-out rates among female students, it would be necessary to tackle the issue of pregnancies directly.

A COURSE OF ACTION

One idea that captured the attention of the superintendent was student clinics in middle and high schools. Such clinics were now becoming involved in issues such as birth control, prenatal care, and child care. Dr. Ochman and Dr. Natali decided to visit two school systems where clinics were operating. Both were located in major metropolitan areas.

Discussion with the principals in schools where these clinics were located produced a number of positive comments. Dr. Ochman was especially interested in determining how the operations were received by the faculty and community. Both principals they visited indicated that only minor problems were encountered and that most teachers and taxpayers were supportive of what they were doing.

On returning to Shelton, Dr. Ochman arranged a meeting solely with community agency directors. He wanted to know if the hospital, the family planning agency, and the mental health clinic would support the schools in the clinic effort. He was told that such support was forthcoming.

The issue of student clinics was introduced to the school board during the May meeting. The superintendent informed the board of what had occurred and indicated that he was preparing a detailed recommendation that would be presented to the board no later than the July meeting. There were no questions or discussion.

The day after the board meeting, Superintendent Ochman met with his four high school principals, the assistant superintendent for instruction, and Dr. Natali. He informed them of his intention to move forward to establish clinics in the four high schools. He further noted that (1) he did not intend to establish such clinics in middle schools at this time, and (2) the clinics would operate under agreements with the county mental health agency, the city hospital, and the welfare department. These agencies would have a linkage and provide support services when necessary.

Two of the principals reacted negatively, indicating they thought this was a mistake. One principal said he welcomed the challenge, and the fourth principal offered no comments.

Despite two principals objecting, Dr. Ochman prepared the following recommendation for the June board meeting:

<u>Superintendent's Recommendation:</u> That a student health clinic be established to provide assistance for students with a variety of health and emotional problems at each of the four high schools. Such problems will include drug and alcohol abuse and teenage pregnancies.

The background information provided by the superintendent outlined the proposed linkages with other community agencies and noted that four directors of these centers would need to be employed. The total budget for operating the clinics for the upcoming year was set at $257,000.

The reaction of the school board members was swift. Three of the seven members immediately voiced opposition to the idea. Board member Tony Copamagi was perhaps the most adamant,

"I don't have problems helping kids who have trouble with drugs. But no way are we going to be getting in the business of running a birth control clinic. This proposal is just too vague about what is going to be done in the area of birth control and pregnancies. Are we going to be giving out free condoms?"

Dr. Ochman responded that these questions were so specific that he could not answer them at this time. He indicated that the clinics would evolve once they were operational and that the board would monitor what occurred.

One supporter of the measure, Mrs. Velma Jackson, became concerned that the measure would go down to defeat immediately. She recommended that the matter be tabled. The vote was four to three to table, with the three declared opponents not even wanting to delay a vote on the issue itself.

The morning after the June board meeting, the *Shelton Daily Examiner*, the local newspaper, carried an editorial against the creation of the clinics. It was the first official act of opposition to come from an organization in the community and it was followed by a myriad of others.

During the three weeks after the June board meeting, Dr. Ochman was inundated with letters opposing the creation of the clinics. A fourth board member had publicly indicated that he probably could not support the idea. The newspaper also reported that at least two of the four high school principals were opposed to the clinics.

Two of the board members who already had declared opposition to the clinics visited Dr. Ochman and pleaded that he withdraw the recommendation. They supported him as superintendent and they did not want to see him destroyed by this controversy. Even his three top assistants suggested privately that he retreat.

Community encouragement for the clinics came mainly from officials in the agencies that were willing to be partners in the venture. There were several parents who wrote to the newspaper editor indicating support for the initiative, but their letters were outnumbered about five to one by communications coming from opponents.

The time had arrived to prepare the July board packets and Dr. Ochman arranged to have lunch with David Potter, the board president. Mr. Potter was a juvenile judge in Shelton and one of two board members who had not stated a position on this matter. The board president told the superintendent that he would try to support any recommendation that he would make. But he also warned him that he did not think that the recommendation for establishing the clinics would be approved. Furthermore, Judge Potter suggested that he would do everything he could to see that this matter did not destroy the superintendent's ability to be an effective leader.

THE CHALLENGE: Place yourself in Dr. Ochman's position. Would you withdraw the recommendation, insist that the board act on it at the July meeting, or propose another solution?

KEY ISSUES/QUESTIONS:

1. Relate the community to this problem. Does the nature of the community have any special influence on this case?
2. Identify the issues that make student health clinics controversial.
3. Evaluate the procedures employed by Dr. Ochman in reaching his recommendation in this matter. Do you believe he was influenced by his own values and beliefs?
4. Identify the advantages and disadvantages of the superintendent:
   a. insisting that his recommendation be acted on at the July board meeting, and
   b. withdrawing his recommendation in order to spare the board the necessity of voting on the matter.
5. Are data concerning the relationship between pregnancies and drop-out rates in Shelton typical for the United States? What are the figures in your school district?
6. How much emphasis would you place on the information collected when the two school officials visited health clinics in other cities?
7. Should board members have stated their positions on this matter prior to a formal vote being taken?
8. Should a superintendent withdraw recommendations when it is obvious that there is no chance they will be approved?
9. Do you think that linkages with community agencies are a good idea? Why or why not?

SUGGESTED READINGS:

Berger, M. (1982). The public schools can't do it all. *Contemporary Education, 54*(1), 6–8.
Bowers, L. (1985). *Religion and education: A study of the interrelationship between fundamentalism and education in contemporary America.* Unpublished Ed.D. thesis, East Tennessee State University.
Buie, J. (1987). Schools must act on teen pregnancy. *The School Administrator, 44*(8), 12–15.
Buie, J. (1987). Teen pregnancy: It's time for schools to tackle the problem. *Phi Delta Kappan, 68*(10), 737–739.
Cook, L. (1987). This proposed health clinic triggered a rhetorical meltdown. *American School Board Journal, 174*(5), 27–28.
Cuban, L. (1988). A fundamental puzzle of school reform. *Phi Delta Kappan, 70*(5), 341–344.

Edwards, L., & Brent, N. (1987). Grapple with those tough issues before giving that clinic the go ahead. *American School Board Journal, 174*(5), 25–27.

Ennis, T. (1987). Prevention of pregnancy among adolescents: Part I, the school's role. *School Law Bulletin, 18*(2), 1–15.

Frymier, J., & Gansneder, B. (1989). The Phi Delta Kappa study of students at risk. *Phi Delta Kappan, 71*(2), 142–146.

Hahn, A. (1987). Reaching out to America's dropouts: What to do? *Phi Delta Kappan, 69*(4), 256–263.

Kirby, D., & Lovick, S. (1987). School-based health clinics. *Educational Horizons, 65*(3), 139–143.

Norris, B. (1985). High school pregnancy clinic survives storm. *Times Educational Supplement, 3617* (October 25), 17.

Peng, S. (1987). Effective high schools: What are the attributes? In J. Land & H. Waldberg (Eds.), pp. 89–108. *Effective school leadership*. Berkeley, CA: McCutcheon.

Ravitch, D. (1982). The new right and the schools: Why mainstream America is listening to our critics. *American Teacher, 6*(3), 8–13, 46.

Schwartz, D., & Darabi, K. (1986). Motivations for adolescents' first visit to a family planning clinic, *Adolescents, 21*, 535–545.

Will, S., & Brown, L. (1988). School-based health clinics: What role? *American Teacher, 72*(3), 4.

CASE 25

A Matter of Honor

THE COMMUNITY

Newton, Michigan, has fallen on hard times during the 1980s. The local economy, once sustained by two automobile-related operations, a transmission plant and a battery plant, has declined markedly. Union strife, lower domestic automobile sales, and automation contributed to massive lay-offs in recent years. The parent companies of the two manufacturing plants decided to divert much of the work from Newton factories to Mexico where the work could be completed more economically. This industrial retrenchment spawned an exodus of citizens, and the city's population dropped from 45,500 to slightly over 38,000 in the past nine years.

During the 1950s, Newton grew rapidly. A steady stream of new residents, especially from southern states, were attracted by the high salaries in the auto-related industries. The community quickly became a mixture of many values and beliefs. There were descendants of eastern European immigrants who moved from large cities seeking better paying jobs. The migration of workers from the deep south included both blacks and whites. The city also attracted a fair number of Hispanics who seasonally would come to Michigan to perform migrant farm work but who were enticed to stay permanently to work in the factories.

The vast majority of the labor force was employed in auto-related industries, so the workers' union emerged as a potent political, social, and economic force in the community. During the prosperous years, organized labor could exercise its influence over many things. In addition to its traditional role of protecting work rights and negotiating contracts, the union proved to be a powerful force in easing racial tensions, creating friendships that crossed ethnic lines, and helping to build integrated neighborhoods and schools. The union provided a common affiliation for many of the Newton residents. When jobs started to disappear, circa 1983, the union started to lose much of its influence. Membership dropped, those remaining in the organization began mistrusting each other, and reduced revenues curtailed the union's social programs (e.g., the union no longer sponsored a Christmas party for the children).

Newton was changing and its people were changing. There was skepticism and in some cases, a defeatist attitude. Taxpayers were less tolerant of initiatives proposed by public agencies; conflicts occasionally took on racial overtones; small businesses started to close; and parents became increasingly concerned about the future of their children.

In 1988, the town elected Stanley Diviak as its mayor. Stanley was 63 years old. From 1965 to 1978, he was president of the local auto workers' union. Many associated his leadership with the "good" years. Some continued to believe that had he stayed in the position of union president, the transmission and battery plants would still be thriving enterprises. Following his election, Mayor Diviak appointed many of his former union associates to key positions in the city administration. He took great care to balance these appointments so that city officials represented the various ethnic and racial groups living in Newton.

THE SCHOOL DISTRICT

The Newton School District is best known for the successes of its high school's athletic teams. The trophy case overflows with evidence of numerous victories in boys' and girls' sports. Principal Nick Furtoski is considered a walking authority on the school's athletic program. He played football for Newton High in the 1950s and helped the school earn its first state gridiron championship. He loves to tell visitors about the seven graduates of Newton High School currently playing professional sports and the average of twenty-three athletes that receive athletic scholarships to continue their education each year. But even Principal Furtoski realizes that the best days are now over.

The high school has lost about one-fourth of its enrollment in the past decade. Overall the school district has declined from about 8,500 students to just over 6,000 students. Superintendent Andrew Sposis has survived seven difficult years as the chief executive of the school district. He has successfully recommended the closing of three schools. He has had to live through annual reductions in force. Since 1985, there have been two teacher strikes and one strike by the custodians' union.

Virtually all of the administrators in Newton obtained their positions through internal promotions. In fact, Superintendent Sposis has never worked in another school district. Over the past twenty-nine years, he has been a teacher, elementary school principal, assistant superintendent for business, and now superintendent.

The school board is composed of five members selected through nonpartisan elections. Members serve three-year terms. Since 1983, the entire board has changed. The current board consists of the following members:

- Casimir Barchek, postal worker
- Yolanda Cody, nurse
- Matthew Miskiewicz, tool and die maker
- Angela Sanchez, housewife
- Darnell Turner, dentist

Mr. Miskiewicz is president of the board and Dr. Turner is the vice-president.

THE INCIDENT

Nancy Allison is a senior at Newton High School. She is a "B" student, an outstanding athlete, one of the most popular students in the school, and she is black. It has been quite a senior year for Nancy. She has been named all-state in basketball and track and has been deluged with scholarship offers from over forty universities. She was elected homecoming queen. But the highlight of the year came on March 1. On that day a special delivery letter arrived from Annapolis, Maryland. The communication notified Nancy that she had received an appointment to the U.S. Naval Academy.

The news of Nancy's appointment spread throughout the town of Newton. No student at the school had ever before received an appointment to one of the service academies. Her picture appeared on the front page of the local newspaper above the story outlining her accomplishments and intentions to accept the appointment. In this depressed community, Nancy's selection for the Naval Academy was hailed as good news.

Within two weeks, Nancy's life was to take a dramatic turn. On the morning of March 12, Janice Durnitz, an English teacher at Newton High School, asked for an emergency appointment with the principal. Mr. Furtoski was summoned from the cafeteria by his secretary and told that the teacher insisted on seeing him immediately. On returning to his office, the principal greeted his visitor with his usual smile.

"Good afternoon, Janice. What could be so important as to take me away from my lunch?" he asked.

"I've got serious and bad news," she responded.

The smile left the administrator's face and he motioned for Janice to enter his office. Once inside, he quickly shut the door.

Janice did not even sit down before saying, "Nancy Allison is in my honors English class and up until last week was doing quite well."

"Well, what's the problem?" inquired the principal.

"One requirement of honors English is to complete a paper on a contemporary novel. The assignment was given to the students at the beginning of the semester. Two days ago was the deadline for submitting an extended outline of the paper. Nancy was the last one in class to submit her work. In fact, she turned it in one day late. I read her outline last night, and I think we have a serious problem."

"Well, exactly what is this problem?" Mr. Furtoski inquired.

"There is no doubt that Nancy is guilty of plagiarism. The material in her outline clearly verifies this," responded the teacher. "I checked it carefully."

"You are absolutely sure about this?" asked the principal. "It could just be a coincidence."

"It's not coincidence," asserted Mrs. Durnitz. "The material comes straight from a review that appeared in a weekly magazine three months ago. I checked three times hoping that I would find some evidence that it was a coincidence. I'm afraid it's plagiarism and school district policy clearly states that a student caught plagiarizing automatically fails the course."

Mr. Furtoski was obviously shaken by the teacher's revelation. A pained look came over his face and he seemed to stare off into space as if not knowing what to say next. Finally, he broke the silence.

"Well, what do you plan to do about this situation?" he asked.

"I have no choice, Nick. Nancy has to fail the course. That's the policy," she answered.

"Janice, we have worked together for over fifteen years. We have never had a student at Newton High School flunk a course because of plagiarism. Hell, half the people in this town don't even know what the word means. Isn't there some way we can seek an alternative? Couldn't we just discipline her and let her make up the work?" the administrator inquired.

"Look, Nick. This student cheated. She has to be punished. If that means she doesn't get into the Naval Academy, that's her fault. She should have thought about that before she copied someone else's work." With those parting comments, the teacher turned and walked out of the principal's office.

Mr. Furtoski was frantic. He shut the door and immediately called the superintendent. As he waited for Andrew Sposis to come on the line, he tried to determine his position in this matter. In those seconds while he waited, the principal decided to support the teacher. When the superintendent came on the line, he was told about the problem and Mr. Furtoski said with conviction, "As much as this hurts me, Andy, I have to go along with the teacher. The student has to get an 'F.' "

The superintendent requested a full report, and after receiving it he conducted a hearing as prescribed by school district policy. The student, her parents and attorney, the principal, and the teacher attended the hearing. The superintendent served as the hearing officer. After listening to the evidence, the superintendent decided to support the prescribed punishment. The parents were furious. They took the story to the local newspaper and immediately leveled charges of racism at the three white educators who were key figures in the case (the teacher, the principal, and the superintendent).

The school board was briefed on the matter in executive session two days following the hearing. The board was divided three to two, with the majority supporting the position of the superintendent to fail the student. The two dissenting board members joined the parents in suggesting to the media that racial issues may possibly be involved in the case. One week later the parents filed a lawsuit against the three educators and the school board.

The issue of Nancy Allison became a heated debate throughout the community. The school district's attorney, Deloris VanSilten, familiarized herself with the matter. Although she did not suggest that the school officials change their position, she repeatedly hinted that the parents could win the suit. Three weeks after initiating legal action, the parents, through their attorney, offered a compromise. They would withdraw the lawsuit if Nancy would be allowed to take an incomplete grade and take the course over with another teacher. Phillip Jones, a member of the English department and a black, offered to assume the task of providing an independent study alternative for Nancy at night so that she could graduate on time.

The board president called an executive session and instructed the superintendent to have the principal present. The board president restated the offer made by Mr. and Mrs. Allison. Then he looked at the principal and asked,

"Nick, what do you think?" We don't want to leave you hanging, but this compromise may be best for everyone." Mr. Furtoski sat there and contemplated how he should respond. He looked over at the superintendent in hopes that he might receive some cue. Mr. Sposis avoided eye contact and just stared at the floor.

THE CHALLENGE: Place yourself in the principal's position. What would you do?

KEY ISSUES/QUESTIONS:

1. Identify the possible alternatives that the principal may pursue in this matter. Evaluate the merits of each.
2. Do you think the teacher could have been more flexible in this matter?
3. To what extent do you think the economic environment of the school district (the community) affects this situation?
4. Is the fact that Newton is a "union" town important to this case? Would the situation be any different if it occurred in a wealthy suburb of Detroit?
5. Most of the administrators in Newton acquired their positions via internal promotions. Do you think this has any bearing on this case?
6. Was the principal correct in immediately deciding to side with the teacher in this matter when he contacted the superintendent? What, if anything, would you have done differently after first learning about the charges of plagiarism?
7. To what extent would your decision on whether to accept the parent's proposal be predicated on the fact that the board is divided on this issue?
8. Can you think of any possible solutions other than the one proposed by the parents?
9. If you were the superintendent, how would you react in this matter?
10. Should growing community tensions play any part in this decision? Why or why not?

SUGGESTED READINGS:

Browlee, G. (1987). Coping with plagiarism requires several strategies. *Journalism Educator, 41*(4), 25–29.

Dant, D. (1986). Plagiarism in high school: A survey. *English Journal, 75*(2), 81–84.

Drum, A. (1986). Responding to plagiarism. *College Composition and Communication, 37*(2), 241–243.

Fass, R. (1986). By honor bound: Encouraging academic honesty. *Educational Record, 67*(4), 32–36.

Geosits, M., & Kirk, W. (1983). Sowing the seeds of plagiarism. *Principal, 62,*(5), 35–38.

Jackson, L. et al. (1987). Dear teacher, Johnny copied. *Reading Teacher, 41*(1), 22–25. (also in *Education Digest,* February *53*(6), 39–41, 1988).

Martin, B. (1984). Plagiarism and responsibility. *Journal of Tertiary Educational Administration, 6*(2), 183–190.

Peterson, P. (1984). Plagiarism: It can happen to you. *Quill and Scroll, 58*(4), 15.

Sauer, R. (1983). Coping with copiers. *English Journal, 72*(4), 50–52.

Shea, J. (1987). When borrowing becomes burglary. *Currents, 13*(1), 38–42.

Skom, E. (1986). Plagiarism: Quite a rather bad little crime. *AAHE Bulletin,* (October 3), 7.

Subject Index

This index is designed to assist you in locating subject areas addressed in the cases. The subjects listed here include both major and minor topics included in the cases.

TOPIC	RELEVANT CASES
Assistant Principals	5, 9, 12, 20, 22
Assistant Superintendents	1, 5, 6, 7, 9, 11, 14, 15, 16, 21, 22, 24
Bureaucratic Values	2, 5, 6, 9, 11, 13, 14, 16, 19, 21
Central Office Directors	2, 11, 16, 22
Collective Bargaining	2, 9, 16, 19, 23
Communication Problems	1, 3, 5, 6, 8, 9, 10, 11, 13, 14, 16, 21
Community Relations	1, 2, 4, 6, 11, 12, 14, 15, 18, 20, 22, 23, 24, 25
Curriculum and Instruction	3, 4, 6, 11, 15, 18, 25
Decisions, Collaborative Procedures	6, 7, 8, 9, 15, 24
Decisions, Conflict Producing	1, 2, 5, 6, 7, 8, 9, 13, 15, 18, 21, 24, 25
Declining Enrollments	2, 4, 25
Discipline Problems/Procedures	1, 12, 22, 24, 25
Educational Reform Attempts	3, 8, 18
Elementary School	1, 15, 16, 18
Elementary School Principles	1, 6, 8, 13, 15, 18, 19
Employment Problems/Practices	5, 9, 10, 21
Ethical Issues	3, 5, 8, 10, 16, 17, 19, 25
Evaluation, Performance	5, 9, 13, 18
Evalution, Program	3, 6, 15, 18, 22
Financial Management	2, 4, 6, 7, 23
High School	5, 6, 9, 17, 20, 22, 24, 25